Confirmed for Life

Confirmed for Life

Gavin Reid
and
Shelagh Brown

The Bible Reading Fellowship
OPENING THE BIBLE

Text copyright © 1995 Gavin Reid and Shelagh Brown

The authors assert the moral right to be
identified as the authors of this work.

Published by
The Bible Reading Fellowship
Peter's Way, Sandy Lane West
Oxford OX4 5HG
ISBN 0 7459 2523 5
Albatross Books Pty Ltd
PO Box 320, Sutherland
NSW 2232, Australia
ISBN 0 7324 0944 6

First edition 1995
10 9 8 7 6 5 4 3 2 1 0

Contents

Introduction

Confirmation is not the end of something. It is the second landmark of the most important beginning of all. All of us have to begin with God. Usually it is a gradual and gentle process of waking up to things and starting to believe. That's why it is helpful to have some clear marker points that remind us, and those around us, that we really have made up our minds to follow Christ.

Baptism dramatizes the offer of God to us. It is an offer of forgiveness and new life. Confirmation gives us the opportunity to say publicly that we have taken God up on his offer. Confirmation is also the occasion where the congregation pray with the bishop for God's Holy Spirit to be the real 'confirmer' or strengthener of a person's life.

And we need all the strength that God can give us because confirmation is—as a famous leader in the early Church put it—the 'ordination of the laity'. God's call to us is never to be spectators but always to be participants in his non-stop, generation-after-generation work in our world.

It is never easy to be a Christian. It goes against the way most people think and it challenges the way most people live. This book assumes that the reader has just been confirmed and is ready to set out on the adventure of being open about being a Christian in today's world.

We hope this will be a practical book. There are two weeks' Bible readings and comments on St Peter's first letter, and simple frameworks for personal morning and evening prayer which you could use.

We hope that **Confirmed for Life** will introduce you to a spirituality for everyday life, because being a Christian is as much about Mondays as it is about Sundays.

+ Gavin Reid and Shelagh Brown

Turning to Christ

Imagine the big moment in a wedding service. There, at the front of the church, stand the bride and groom, and the minister gets to the point where he asks each the big question: 'Do you take So-and-so to be your wedded husband, or wife…' The mother of the bride dabs a tear from her eyes. The flowers in church are beautiful. The dresses of bride and bridesmaids are magnificent. And in the middle of all this, as the big question is put, everyone hears the answer…

'No—I've changed my mind!'

Of course we don't expect one of the couple to say 'no', but it could happen, and it has happened. It would be wrong to have a wedding service where we take the answers to those questions for granted. Getting married is a big commitment and we need to be sure that both parties are willing for that commitment.

Just in case you, the reader, are beginning to wonder whether you have picked up the wrong book—yes, this *is* a book about confirmation!

At your confirmation you were also asked questions—six of them. In this chapter I want to concentrate on the first three. You were asked these questions for the very same reason that we ask questions in the wedding service—because a big commitment is about to take place. It would be wrong to conduct a confirmation service without making public that the candidates want to go ahead, and that they realize what is involved. Everything else in the service depended on your answer to those questions. Those questions were:

Do you turn to Christ?
Do you repent of your sins?
Do you renounce evil?

The first three questions focus upon your *attitudes*. The second three questions focus on your *understanding*. Both attitudes and understanding are important but there is little point in having the right understanding about something if your attitude is that they are not particularly important.

Let's say that I *understand* that the road tax on my car is out of date but my *attitude* is that I am going to take a chance that I don't get caught out. It won't do me much good, when I'm stopped by a vigilant policeman, to say that I really do *understand* about the need to renew my road tax! That actually makes things worse. It makes me all the more guilty for doing nothing.

With God, it isn't enough to to have the right understanding in our minds. Plenty of people say they believe in God, but that is not enough. If I *know* that he exists and that I ought to be living the way he wants me to live, I am all the more guilty for having a 'couldn't care less' attitude.

Getting confirmed is not a formality. It is not something you do because you have got to a certain age or because relatives think you 'ought' to. It is a commitment and it calls for the right attitude, which means that you take it seriously. That's the attitude we expect from a couple on their wedding day, and that's the attitude that I, as a bishop, expect from the candidates on their confirmation day—total commitment. It doesn't surprise me if the candidates have a long way to go in terms of their *understanding*, but the *attitude* must be right or the whole thing is an empty ceremony and an insult to God himself. Being a committed Christian is very similar to being married—it is about a lifelong relationship.

Do you turn…?

So let me get back to these first three questions. The first one is the big one—*do you turn to Christ?* The other two simply spell out what is involved in turning to Christ. If people turn to Christ, then they simply must, at the same time, repent of their sins and renounce evil. There is no way you can say 'I'm a Christian—I have turned to Christ', and still deliberately carry on doing what is against everything that Christ stands for.

The great challenge of Jesus of Nazareth to the followers of his own day was: 'repent and believe'. The one needs the other. To repent means to turn to a new direction because of a change of mind. That change of mind is the change to believing that Jesus Christ is Lord and must take first place in our priorities. To turn *to* Christ means that we have to turn *away* from whatever used to be the most important thing in our lives.

For some that might have been another set of religious beliefs. For some, it may have been self-centredness. (Let's face it, most of us slip into believing that nothing is more important than ourselves!) For some it may be materialism—believing that possessions are the only things that matter. For many it may mean turning away from merely drifting casually through life.

This is where I think there is a clash between what Christianity actually is, and what so many think it is. They talk as if Christianity is a private opinion, something that you can take on board which may be helpful from time to time. That's why it is so popular to say that 'you don't have to go to church to be a Christian'. The truth of the matter is very different. To become a Christian is to take sides publicly for Jesus

Christ. That is what baptism and confirmation are all about. That is why each candidate is asked: *Do you turn to Christ?* Baptism and confirmation are about joining the local Christian congregation and realizing that it is not a club for those who 'like that sort of thing', but a team of people openly committed to working for Christ's cause. And there's something more. To join the local congregation is to join the worldwide, 2,000-year-old Church of Christ.

To whom do we turn?

The claim we make when we get confirmed is that we have turned *to Christ*. We need to be clear about this. We have not turned to the Church, or to religion, or to the pleasant local congregation (although Christian fellowship is tremendously important). We have not even turned to 'God'. We have turned *to Christ*. At the heart of the Christian faith is this conviction that in Jesus Christ, God has shown us what he is like and how we are to think about him.

The name *Christ* is not a surname like Smith or Jones. It is a title. It means someone who is specially anointed by God himself. When Jesus lived on earth the Jewish people were looking for 'he that should come' and talked about a 'Christ' (or, to use the word in their own language, a *messiah*).

So it is to Jesus that we turn, and here Christians insist on something else. To turn to Jesus is not to become someone who remembers a dead hero or teacher from the past. Christians believe that the Holy Spirit of God brings Jesus into our lives and our experience now. Turning to Christ is turning to a person living now. We learn about his character from the New Testament Gospels written about him, and that same Jesus is with us by his Spirit. It is not stretching things too far to say that we can get to know him and sense his presence.

10

The fact that we can have a relationship with Jesus in the present does not mean that we can ignore what was written about him in the past. The New Testament writings go back to the memories of the very people who lived alongside Jesus while he was on earth. They stored up their memories and passed them on to others, and finally they were written down. Those ancient writers wrote in ways that are different from present-day biographers or news reporters. What we have in the four Gospels (especially in the first three) is a carefully arranged collection of episodes from the life of Jesus plus a collection of sayings. In some ways they wrote as if for a film script or television documentary. The reader is not given a lecture or a list of conclusions about Jesus. Rather he or she is thrown in to experience Jesus at work. We hear him teaching. We see him meeting people—not always friendly. We encounter him healing. We reflect on his teachings to the little group of followers who accompanied him and who were being prepared to carry on his ministry after he had gone.

Above all we are made to be witnesses of his terrible public execution by crucifixion. And no sooner have we faced that unjust and undeserved 'end' to his life than we are taken to the garden tomb where Jesus was buried—only to find it empty. We watch while everyone, friend and foe alike, is thrown into confusion. Jesus appears, here to this group of startled followers, and then there to another. Finally most of the first Christians gather and they see their risen Master taken from them for the last time. The only way they can make sense of what they see is to say that he has 'ascended' to the Father.

This is the story they tell, and we who are Christians believe that it is true and that our whole lives need to be built around the conviction of its truth. Jesus, we believe, is the unique Son of God. He has come into our world and lived among us. He has shown us that God exists as a caring heavenly Father. He has shown that the Father has the power over death and he promised that in our own time we also will survive our deaths, and that there is more, and much better, to come.

Whenever I think about the resurrection of Jesus it raises a question that won't go away. If God could raise his Son, why did he let him die? I believe that the answer to that question was acted out in what is known as the Last Supper, which is re-enacted at every eucharist or communion service. His body was broken *for us*. His blood was *shed for the forgiveness of our sins*.

What is God like?

So what does Jesus show us about the character of God? Quite simply, he shows that God cares about us. That love was so great that he was prepared to come and live among people like us—with all the pains and frustrations of being human. This care and concern is shown in the way Jesus related to people. Take, for example, the famous story of the feeding of the five thousand.

The story begins with huge crowds coming together to hear Jesus teach. They had travelled long distances, and they stayed listening a long time. When it was time for them to go, Jesus began to worry about their welfare.

Our modern minds may boggle at the accounts in the Gospels of the feeding of several thousand people from practically no supplies, but I think that the reason why Jesus worked the miracle is even more astonishing. Unlike modern politicians working the crowds to their own advantage in a promotional campaign, Jesus was worried that some of the people would collapse on their way home—they simply had to be fed! God, I believe, is like that!

Then there were those somewhat superstitious parents who jostled him as he was trying to walk through their village. His followers tried to push them back until Jesus saw that the people wanted him to bless their children. Everything had to stop! 'Let the children come to me—do not stop them' was his call. And the children came. God is like that.

Children, and other disadvantaged or weak people, were very important to the Jesus we read about in the Gospels. On one occasion when Jesus literally had a small child on his knee or at his side, he uttered perhaps the most chilling words he ever spoke:

'…if anyone causes one of these little ones who believe in me to sin, it would be better for him to have a large millstone hung around his neck and to be drowned in the depths of the sea.'

Matthew 18:6

A God who judges

If, as Christians believe, Jesus shows us what God the Father is like, then it is a picture that should both encourage us and disturb us. The God who loves children and who cares about the weak is a God who judges those who hurt others. One of the parables of Jesus brings out this sterner side. He told a story about a day of judgment in which people would be separated into two groups just as the shepherds of his day would separate sheep from goats. One of these groups would be welcomed by God; the other would be rejected and go away to 'eternal punishment'.

The issue upon which judgment would rest was what those being judged had actually done with their lives and what effect they had made on others—especially the weak. Christ's words are striking:

' "… I was hungry and you gave me something to eat, I was thirsty and you gave me something to drink, I was a

*stranger and you invited me in, I needed clothes and you
clothed me, I was sick and you looked after me, I was in
prison and you came to visit me."*

*'Then the righteous will answer him, "Lord, when did we
see you hungry and feed you, or thirsty and give you
something to drink? When did we see you a stranger and
invite you in, or needing clothes and clothe you…?"*

*'The King will reply, "I tell you the truth, whatever you
did for one of the least of these brothers of mine, you did for
me." '*

Matthew 25:35–40

What these words make clear is that Jesus shows
God to be far from the caricature of a jolly Father
Christmas in the sky. There is a chilling holiness about
him. There is a profound seriousness in him. He doesn't
just talk about judgment. He *is* judgment! To be in his
presence is to hear a voice saying 'guilty' or 'not guilty'.
And the astonishing thing is that the voice that
pronounces sentence is one's own voice.

Perhaps too many of us who call ourselves
Christians take God too lightly. Jesus, for all the non-
stop kindliness of his life, frequently talked about a day
of judgment. So we see these two different and yet
related sides to the character of God when we reflect on
Jesus. St Paul wrote in one of his famous letters:
'Consider therefore the kindness and sternness of God'
(Romans 11:22).

It is hard to hold these two sides of God's character
together until we go back to the cross of Christ and look
at it in the light of his words at the Last Supper. There
on the cross we see the one who is God's unique Son
dying as a body broken, and blood shed, '… *shed for the
forgiveness of your sins'*. It is this forgiveness, and the fact
that it was bought with the very death of Christ, that
makes us feel able to look to God with hope and
assurance. We see both the kindness and the sternness

of God demonstrated on the cross. As St John, in his mysterious Fourth Gospel, said so powerfully:

God so loved the world that he gave his one and only Son, that whoever believes in him shall not perish but have eternal life.

John 3:16

It is to this Jesus Christ that we turn. He has shown us that God is real and that he is not to be taken lightly. He has also shown us that this same heavenly Father has a deep love for all of us—a love that led Jesus himself to be rejected and persecuted in his life and die a cruel death *for each one of us*. He has made it possible for everyone and anyone to be a friend of God, no matter what sort of life they may have lived. To turn to Christ is to pin all your hopes on this forgiveness and the new standing in God's eyes that it brings. It is to be saved from sin. It is to become a child of God.

But this turning is to a Lord who is alive! Jesus Christ is not some sort of heavenly insurance policy. We are turning to someone who calls us to be his physical presence in a hurting world. There are still children who need blessing and protecting. There are still those who are hungry and thirsty. There are still the destitute who need help and hope. And there are still those in prison who, quite literally, need visiting. And whatever we try to do for such people, we will find we are doing to and for Jesus himself.

To turn to Christ is to take sides with him.

How do I turn?

It was no problem for the disciples in the Gospel stories to 'turn to Christ'. They could see him! When he gave his famous call to 'follow me' it was a simple matter to obey. How do we today do our turning and following when there is no physical Jesus standing in front of us?

Some things, in fact, have not changed. When the first disciples turned to Jesus, they didn't act like zombies. They thought about it—however quickly—and they decided. The same starting point remains in place for us today. We cannot drift into turning to and following Christ. We may drift a fair part of the way towards taking sides with him. We may be happy to be in the company of others who are following Christ. What we cannot do, without making a clear-cut decision, is to turn to him. At some point in our lives there comes a time when we have to agree within ourselves that following Christ is what we want to do.

The confirmation service could be such a moment, but in the vast majority of cases those who want to be confirmed, especially if they are adults, do so because they have already agreed within themselves that they want to turn to Christ.

There is a second point of similarity between turning to Christ then and now. When Jesus called people to turn to him, he called them to join the ranks of his followers. He didn't have a number of independent, solitary followers—he had a group of followers. He taught them as a group. He gave them different jobs to do and he used them as a team.

That is exactly what a church is all about. Turning to Christ has to mean joining a church. In a church we are a group of followers. In a church we learn about Christ. In a church we are encouraged to use our differing gifts. In a church we are meant to work as a team for Christ's sake.

There is a third similarity between someone who had turned to Christ in the times of the Bible and in the present day. The follower was known as a 'disciple'. That means that he or she was a *learner*.

To turn to Christ and to follow him today means to want to be a learner. St Paul talked of people who 'learn Christ' (Ephesians 4:20, see AV, RSV and NRSV). This is something more than simply learning *about* Christ. It is about coming to know what he is like because, through prayer and through Bible study, and through the work of the Holy Spirit, you have actually begun to know him directly.

So we turn to Christ through:

1. **making a decision to turn to him**
2. **joining a church**
3. **devoting ourselves to 'learn' him.**

What do we turn from?

To turn to Christ means to turn from whatever else has taken first place in our lives. There's an old saying that states: *If he's not Lord of all, he's not Lord at all.*

This is what repentance is all about. It is not about being emotional or even 'sorry'. It is about making up our minds to turn away from whatever else took first place, so that Jesus Christ can be our Lord and Leader. Much of what we must turn from is not particularly wrong. It is only wrong if it keeps us from putting Christ first. It's not wrong to have money but it becomes wrong if we put money before everything else. It is most certainly not wrong to love one's family, but even that can be wrong if we put our family before Christ. He must come first, but he calls us to live loving and unselfish lives and he calls us to treasure our relationships—so our family is going to be all right in any case!

There are, however, some things that touch our lives which are evil—positively evil. They are totally against the wishes of a loving, pure and unselfish God. They are hurtful and destructive. If we are to turn to Christ we must positively *renounce* such things.

To renounce something is to decide to have absolutely nothing to do with it. That is easy to say in a confirmation service. It is far more difficult to do if there is an evil practice that is not only part of your life, but part of some practice at work which everybody does. A true story may bring this home.

John (we shall call him that) worked for a small but high-powered partnership who worked as consultants to industry. John joined the firm soon after turning to Christ. He soon found that his fellow partners were fiddling their expenses and claiming well beyond what they had spent in the strict line of duty. John did not feel that he could do that, so his expense returns told the truth. His returns showed that he had spent far less than his partners even though he was doing the same job. His expense returns showed them in a bad light. There was only one thing that the company could do. Either the other partners had to go, or John would have to go for revealing that they were dishonest. John was told to leave.

To renounce evil is not always easy but it is always right. We must not assume that God will in some way protect us from the unpleasant consequences of renouncing some evil when one is in a set-up where 'everyone does it'. But it is always right to do so, and in the long run we need to believe that God will not let us down.

It is not easy to turn to Christ when one is surrounded by those who haven't and don't appear to want to. Sometimes the follower of Christ becomes very aware of the reality of evil. To turn to Christ is to take sides with him and there are plenty of people who deliberately, or without realizing it, are taking sides against him.

In some countries the very laws of the land are opposed to Christ and Christian values. Jesus never said it would be easy. He talked of 'taking up the cross and following him' and in saying that he was using a phrase that pictured the way condemned prisoners were made to carry the cross on which they would be executed through the streets to the place where they would die.

It's all a far cry from the popular caricature of church life as a quaint, gentle business which appeals only to rather odd and inadequate people. It is certainly true that our loving God welcomes the quaint and the odd and the inadequate. Every true church should have people like that. But the call to turn to Christ is a rugged business and the amazing thing is that in the first days of the Christian Church when there was persecution and the killing of Christians, St Paul could write: '...God chose the foolish things of the world to shame the wise; God chose the weak things of the world to shame the strong' (1 Corinthians 1:27).

He doesn't change!

2

Believing and trusting

I once heard a story about an elderly man taking his first air trip. As he looked around at the sheer size of the airliner, and at the large number of passengers, he became increasingly worried about the weight that was about to be lifted into the skies and kept up there during the flight.

He decided to help. He lifted his feet off the floor and, with great difficulty, kept them off the floor for the duration of the flight! He hoped that this would at least reduce the payload to the tune of his eleven stone something.

I have a great deal of sympathy for that man. I don't often fly, but whenever I do I never cease to be amazed at what is going on. The sheer size of a wide-bodied, long-haul airliner is breathtaking. Its weight, when loaded, must be enormous.

Yet although I find it difficult to understand fully about such things as 'lift' and aerodynamics, I believe that jumbo jets can fly, and when I get on board I show that I trust that they can. Because of my belief, and my experiences of trusting jumbo jets, I can easily say that I know that such large aircraft can fly. I have been in them several times on long journeys. They really can take off and stay up! I believe and trust, and as a result of my experience of trusting, I know.

The second three questions which are put to the candidates in a confirmation service are about believing and trusting:

Do you believe and trust in God the Father who made the world?

Do you believe and trust in his Son Jesus Christ who redeemed mankind?

Do you believe and trust in his Holy Spirit who gives life to the people of God?

The candidates are not being asked whether they believe in God in the same way that they might believe that the world is round. Our English word 'believe' is not a very strong one. When public opinion pollsters go out and ask whether people 'believe in God', and when seven out of ten people say 'yes', what most of them are talking about is a sort of recognition that there probably is a God of some sort. What the confirmation questions are about is the sort of believing that you need when you get on board an airliner. It is the believing that leads to action. Christians are far more than believers, *they are trusters*. Trusting is about the way we live as well as the way we think. When a Christian says 'I believe in God' he or she means 'I am basing my life on what I believe.'

A mind-boggling God

The three questions and the answers we give do not make things easy for us. One moment we are talking about God as Father. That is perhaps the easiest picture to get hold of. The next moment we are talking about God as Son. That, for many, is far harder to grasp. Finally, to keep things complicated, we find ourselves saying that we believe and trust 'in his Holy Spirit who gives life to the people of God'.

What all this points up is the mysterious Christian doctrine of the Holy Trinity. It is a teaching about God which is unique among world religions. Christians believe that there is one God, and yet there are three 'persons' within the oneness.

First we become aware of the Creator God. The thought of God as 'Father' is hardly ever used in the Old Testament books, but there is no doubting that God is Creator and that he deeply concerns himself in the affairs of human beings—particularly with regard to the people of Israel who are marked out to be a nation that bears witness to him. When Jesus comes onto the scene, however, there is a dramatic difference. The thought of God as 'Father' is on practically every page of the New Testament. God, he would say, is 'our Father'. To pray is to talk to a caring, heavenly Father.

However, Jesus does more than talk repeatedly about a heavenly Father. He talks with a note of authority that no other religious teacher dared to do. Even more, he goes so far as to take it upon himself to pronounce forgiveness upon those who are conscious of their sins. Some religious teachers heard him doing this on one occasion and muttered amongst themselves, 'who can forgive sins but God only?' They were more right than they realized!

The reason why Jesus fell foul of the religious authorities of his day was that he claimed more than they believed any man had the right to claim. The crunch came when Jesus was put on trial in a religious court. In Matthew's Gospel the matter comes to a head:

The high priest said to [Jesus], 'I charge you under oath by the living God: Tell us if you are the Christ, the Son of God. 'Yes, it is as you say,' Jesus replied. 'But I say to all of you: In the future you will see the Son of Man sitting at the right hand of the Mighty One and coming on the clouds of heaven.' Then the high priest tore his clothes and said, 'He has spoken blasphemy! Why do we need any more witnesses? Look, now you have heard the blasphemy. What do you think?' 'He is worthy of death,' they answered.

Matthew 26:63–66

There is no escaping this side to the picture of Jesus in the New Testament. Those who want to describe Jesus merely as a religious teacher or leader need to recognize that the only historical evidence that we have for him speaks of a miracle worker who forgave people's sins and accepted their worship, and who, after death and burial, was raised from the grave. The first Christians were clear that Jesus was Son of God and God himself—and those first Christians came from a tradition that strongly believed that there was one God.

However, the story gets even more complicated! John's Gospel contains sections where Jesus speaks of 'another comforter', namely the Holy Spirit. There are two words for 'other' in the original language of the New Testament writers. One of those words means 'another of the same sort' and the other means 'another of a different sort'. The word used in John's Gospel means 'another of the same sort'.

So the Holy Spirit is 'of the same sort' as Jesus. He is to be regarded as equally important as God the Son and God the Father! The whole thing is very strange if not ridiculous, but in some way the very oddness of this historic Christian belief in the 'three-and-yet-one-God' gives it some credibility. Who would ever want to invent such an odd idea? When you read the New Testament it becomes clear that the first Christians talked in these strange ways *because it was the only way to describe what they had experienced*.

We must not allow the oddness of this belief in the Trinity to worry us. There are several things that we take for granted in life which are beyond our understanding. *Time* and *space* are typical. We don't understand them, yet we use the ideas of time and space as if we did. For example, built into the idea of space is the fact that there is an outside to every inside! So what is outside outside? The mind boggles! Again, built into the idea of time is the fact that everything has a before and an after. Very well then—what is before before?

We don't understand time and space but we know we are talking about the real world when we talk about time and space. In the same way, all talk about God, especially in this business about the Trinity, is at the very edge of our experience. But that does not, and that must not, stop us talking about God. It should not surprise us that he is beyond our ability to understand him.

And when we can get beyond the oddness of talk about the Trinity, it opens up some very exciting and encouraging thoughts. Some of these are to be found in the wording of the second set of questions.

God the Father

What, then, is so encouraging about believing that God is the Father who made the world?

For me, the most exciting thing about such a belief is that it makes sense of the world and it makes sense of me! Christians differ amongst themselves about the mechanics of creation. Most accept the evidence that a long evolutionary process took place to get us to where we are. Some want to insist that the early chapters of Genesis should be taken more literally. The point that really matters, however, is not how God made the world, but why he did. What becomes clear from the Bible is that God is someone who simply must love others—so there have to be others to love! Perhaps this threeness in the Trinity gives us a clue to God's profound need to be in fellowship with other persons.

What comes across so powerfully in the opening chapters of the Bible is the care that God took to put together an environment that would support human beings and enable them to flourish. God is pictured as

24

a creator and as a quality controller. At every step of creation, as the whole infrastructure for human life is put together, the phrase is repeated—'and God saw that it was good'.

Today as we study the universe it becomes increasingly obvious that the planet earth has a uniqueness in the way that it can support the sort of sophisticated life forms that abound. Our scientists cannot say why this is the case, but the Bible can. It says that God made it that way so that human beings can flourish and live in fellowship with their heavenly Father.

And how magnificent a creation is the human being! The brain is so compact, yet it can put the most sophisticated electronic computing equipment to shame. Look at a hand and the astonishing range of functions it can perform! And then there is the whole matter of beauty and handsomeness and our ability to recognize and enjoy these qualities.

We do not live in a merely functional world. Everywhere you look there is beauty. We see it in birds, flowers, animals, trees, the colours of mountains and skies. Whoever made the world most certainly 'saw that it was good'.

In recent years we have become more and more aware that human beings are making a good world into a bad one. We are polluting the physical environment and many of us would add that we are also polluting the moral environment. If we return to those simple creation accounts at the beginning of the Bible we will discover some clues as to the reasons for this polluting. The second chapter of the book of Genesis (which means 'beginnings') talks, simply, in gardening terms:

The Lord God took the man and put him in the Garden of Eden to work it and take care of it.

Genesis 2:15

It is clear that men and women are meant to be the guardians of the planet earth and that God expects us to care for the environment, which, in turn, cares for us.

To believe and trust in God the Father is to realize that we are on the receiving end of an immense amount of unselfish love. It was the unselfishness of God's love that led to men and women being made in his image—free to choose to love back. The tragic story so simply put in the third chapter of Genesis is that, from the very start of human history, men and women abused that freedom and made other choices—selfish choices. We, in our own time, are the inheritors of endless generations of human beings who are long out of the habit of seeing themselves as answerable to their heavenly Father and responsible for the care of the planet. We are the victims of these past 'sins' but we, alas, also repeat them in our own lives.

To trust in the Father is to believe that, in spite of all that may be wrong on the human side of the fence, he is still the same. He longs to have people to love. He still wants us to enjoy his creation and each other. He still looks to us to take responsibility for the beautiful planet earth.

And, above all, he wants us to know that each one of us is here because he wants us here. Each one of us matters. The world is not an accident and neither are we!

God the Son

Believing and trusting in God the Son, Jesus Christ, *'who redeemed mankind'* is what makes a Christian a Christian. It is what marks him or her out from those who belong to the Jewish and Muslim faiths who also believe in God as a creator.

The most exciting thing about Jesus is that we didn't dream him up. We do not believe in him because some teachers thought out this idea of a Son of God, but because in first-century Palestine people were confronted with him. In Jesus we believe God came to us and showed himself. It was yet another demonstration of the love of the Father and his need to be in relationship with the persons he created.

Christianity is not something that has been reasoned out. The oddness of the Trinity is proof that we haven't worked out some teaching that fits with our powers of reasoning. Christianity is based on what God has revealed or shown to us. We believe that God, in the person of his Son, deliberately came into our world to do something about the mess that endless generations of selfish human beings had made of things.

Of course all this is mind-boggling—just as we have seen that the concepts of time and space are. Christians believe that God became a man, starting with the experience of being born and growing up as a child exactly as any other human being does. The Gospels tell us little about his childhood. Two of the four do not even mention it. All take it as hugely important that he became a man. All record his ministry of teaching, healing and gathering a new community of followers. All make clear that his crucifixion was no accident or tragedy but at the very centre of what he was all about. All agree that God raised him from the dead and that if this had not happened Jesus would not be good news.

St Paul summed up the meaning of Jesus in the words: 'God was reconciling the world to himself in Christ, not counting men's sins against them' (2 Corinthians 5:19). The whole story of Jesus is about God making peace with the people of the world, a peace that comes as a result of the life and death of Jesus.

The peace offer is powerfully expressed in the communion service or eucharist. At the heart of that service we re-enact the Last Supper when Jesus took bread, broke it and said 'this is my body', and then took a cup of wine saying 'this is my blood'. It is critically important to realize that the thing Jesus most wanted to be remembered by was this simple act of eating bread and drinking wine, knowing that it stands for his body and his blood. We now understand what the disciples at the Last Supper could not have understood at the time. Jesus, in this simple action with bread and wine, was explaining the meaning of what was to happen the next day when he was bustled to a place of execution and nailed up on the cross to die.

You cannot make sense of the cross unless you look at it through the 'eyes' of the Last Supper. His body was broken for us and his blood shed for the forgiveness of our sins. His death was not an accident or something that went wrong. His death was at the heart of what those words of St Paul were about. His death was at the centre of the task of reconciling a holy God with his unholy and rebellious people.

Learned and devout Christian thinkers over the centuries have tried to spell out theories about what they call 'the atonement' (at-one-ment between God and people). They have tried to explain exactly how the life and death of Jesus bring about our forgiveness and make it possible for the Father to be at peace with his children. I cannot attempt to give a satisfactory answer in a few lines! What I can say, however, is that theories about the atonement are far less important than the atonement itself. The fact is that, because of Jesus and his death for us, we are at one with the Father. All that is called for from us is trust in Jesus.

Trusting leads to knowing. The Christian can say, 'I know I am forgiven.' We can say this, not because we are any better than anyone else, but because we believe and trust that Jesus has put us right with God. And not only can Jesus be the basis for putting us right with God, he can also be the basis for putting us right with each other. St Paul took up this theme in his letter to the Ephesians. He was writing at a time when the world was very conscious of its social and ethnic divisions. He reminded his readers that all fatherhood stemmed originally from God and that Christ had come and had died for everyone. The dividing walls between differing groups were pulled down when Jesus came and died for all of us.

God the Holy Spirit

The final question asked at the confirmation service is: *'Do you believe and trust in his Holy Spirit, who gives life to the people of God?'*

In my experience Christians talk either too little about the Holy Spirit—or too much! It is also very easy to speak of the Spirit as an 'it' or as something that fills us up or pours over our heads. The fact of the matter is that the Holy Spirit is God and should be referred to as 'he'.

In John's Gospel there are some words that help us to see how the Spirit works:

'… when he, the Spirit of truth, comes, he will guide you into all truth. He will not speak on his own; he will speak only what he hears… He will bring glory to me by taking from what is mine and making it known to you.'

John 16:13–14

It is clear that the Holy Spirit is the self-effacing member of the Trinity. He has done his job well when people become conscious of Jesus or of God as Father. Indeed one of the supreme evidences that the Spirit has come into a person's life is for that person to become deeply aware of God as his or her Father. St Paul's words bear this out:

Because you are sons, God sent the Spirit of his Son into our hearts, the Spirit who calls out, 'Abba, Father.'

Galatians 4:6

In one breath the Spirit has been called the 'Spirit of his Son' and in the next we read that the effect the Spirit has is to make people aware of the Father. That is why we need to be careful of talk that is too focused on the Spirit himself. In the last twenty years or so, the Church has been rediscovering the reality of the Holy Spirit after a time of thinking too little about him.

The fact of the matter is that nobody would come to faith in Christ if it was not for the work of the Holy Spirit, nor could anyone be aware of God as Father if the Spirit was not already at work in his or her life. Yet the truth is that most of us live our lives for much of the time as if the Spirit of God was not there to strengthen us and help us to grow more like Christ. It is no bad thing therefore to take stock, to be aware of the closeness of God through his Holy Spirit and to ask him to come in and upon us afresh.

How does the Holy Spirit 'give life to the people of God'? The New Testament suggests two important ways in which this life shows itself. The first is in the giving of spiritual gifts. In the first letter to the Corinthians (where St Paul had to deal with some who were over-enthusiastic about the Spirit) we meet this teaching about God giving us various particular gifts that are meant to be used in his service. These gifts include wisdom, knowledge, healing, faith, prophesy and the ability to praise and pray in a 'tongue' other than one's own. The church in Corinth (like some today) seemed to be over-interested in the more unusual and dramatic of these gifts, but St Paul pointed out that all mattered equally and it was God who decided who was gifted in what way.

I don't believe that the lists of gifts that St Paul gives in a number of places are in any way full lists. I'm sure that God is thinking of new ways in which to give gifts to his children. I also think that some of the gifts are related to natural abilities that a person has, or are even the result of human circumstance—such as wealth. In the letter to the Romans, St Paul lists one of the gifts of the Spirit as 'contributing to the needs of others'. On the other hand, that same list included 'prophesying'. The fact is that the Holy Spirit can touch and transform what we already have or give us some totally new ability. The important thing is to realize that such gifts are not rewards for spiritual progress. They are given to make individual people more able to play their part in the life and witness of the Church as a whole.

We also read, in the New Testament, of the 'fruit of the Spirit':

… the fruit of the Spirit is love, joy, peace, patience, kindness, goodness, faithfulness, gentleness and self-control.
Galatians 5:22

What we are seeing here is something different from the idea of the Spirit generating particular giftings. We are looking at the ability of the Spirit to touch our lives and develop the character of Christ in each one of us. This idea of the fruit of the Spirit is balanced in St Paul's teaching with the parallel of the acts of 'the sinful nature' (some translations describe this as 'the flesh').

The acts of the sinful nature are obvious: sexual immorality, impurity and debauchery; idolatry… hatred, discord, jealousy… factions… drunkenness…
Galatians 5:19–21

When the Spirit of God comes into our lives he does not bring bliss. He brings inner conflict. He opens up an inner tug of war between the old nature in us and the new Christlike nature that he brings. Just as a new baby coming into the family brings joy but also plenty of demands and challenges to your selfishness, so the coming of God's Spirit into a person's life can be disturbing as well as delightful! Nor does the Spirit 'take over'. We are called to cooperate with him and to let him do his work in us. Holiness is something we must want and work for, but it is also something that the Holy Spirit brings as we make room for it.

The most important thing that the Holy Spirit wants to do is to make the Church powerful in sharing and living out its gospel. We are meant to be good-news people—a blessing to those around us. We are meant to be those who make Christ known, and that is something that exactly relates to what the Spirit is all about. He is the 'make-Christ-known' Spirit. If we want to be the 'make-Christ-known' Church, then we will find that he is indeed the one 'who gives life to the people of God'!

3

In good company

When I was nine years of age my parents moved from Scotland to South London. It was during the Second World War and things were far from normal. The move took, in fact, several months to execute. We left Scotland in the spring and finally found a home in November. We had lived with relatives and in a guest house in the meantime and the family was split up for several months.

I knew nobody. My parents arranged for me to go to the nearest school which was, in fact, a Church of England school. With my broad Scottish accent I stood out like a sore thumb! I was pretty lonely.

One day the 'Lady Worker', as they used to be known (this was in the days when no one would have dreamed of ordaining women), visited the school. In the course of the visit she came up to me and we talked. She then said five simple words that changed the whole course of my life.

'You must come to Pathfinders!'

Pathfinders was the name of the Sunday school for under-elevens that was run by a remarkable and caring businessman. He and his grown-up son poured all their spare energies into running a large, noisy and enormously happy Sunday school. As I had nothing better to do on the Sunday following the Lady Worker's visit to school, I went along and since that day I have never stopped 'going to church'. What I discovered that day was more than a Sunday school. I discovered what it was like to be 'in good company'.

In time I graduated to older children's activities, moved on to Bible class and the youth group. After university and national service, I began to train for the ordained ministry. Ordination followed and after thirty-two years in the Church's ministry I was made—for some strange reason—a bishop!

And it all started when an undervalued woman on the staff of a South London church visited the church school, saw my loneliness and invited me to become someone who *belonged*.

And now, all these years later, working as a bishop, what do I see as I look around the churches in the diocese which I serve?

I see over 250 congregations—groups of people who are held together by their faith in the God who showed us what he is like in Jesus Christ. I admit that some of them are far from lively, but many of them are full of life. Many of those congregations have fewer than twenty-five people meeting on a Sunday, with some only in single figures. Our diocese is very rural in places with many tiny villages. Some churches are bigger, with two or three hundred gathering to worship at the Sunday services. A small church, however, is not a failed church, nor is it any less a church than one with a large congregation.

In addition to going to various churches to preach or for special services—such as confirmations—I spend most of a day in about forty parishes every year. I work closely with another bishop who does the same. With every visit we discover that 'Church' is far more than a building where people 'go' to attend services. We discover that the Church is really all about the people themselves. One of our famous Prayer Book prayers describes the Church as 'the blessed company of all faithful people'. Indeed, there are not always special buildings to go to. I can think of three churches which are made up of people who meet for worship in a school. All over the country this is happening. When you count in the number of congregations belonging to other denominations that meet in schools, halls and even cinemas, the number is large. 'Church' is about people—not buildings with stained glass windows.

Again I find that in many churches a great deal is going on outside of the Sunday services. There are small groups meeting in people's houses to pray or to discuss what the Bible has to say. There are groups running activities for parents and toddlers to give young mums a break. There are groups running young people's activities while, at the other end of the scale, meetings for elderly people are run by Christians all over the diocese. Others, in the name of the local church, are visiting and comforting the bereaved. In areas where there are great social needs you will find churches, either separately or in cooperative ways, working to deal with everything from drug abuse to homelessness. In addition to those activities organized by churches, you will find large numbers of Christians, as part of their personal discipleship, working in community welfare activities or giving generously to important charities.

All over the country, and indeed all over the world, Christians stand out for two things. The first is that they gather regularly to worship God and the second is that they disperse at other times into the community to serve God and their fellow men and women. Christians of all denominations have been prominent in famine relief and world development. Historically Christians were involved heavily in the development of hospitals, schools and industrial reform. The movement to end the slave trade was led by Christians. In recent times, the churches played a major part in creating the new South Africa.

Of course there are plenty of failures to live up to these ideals both at local church level and in the personal lives of Christians but the fact is that the 'company of all faithful people' *has these ideals in the first place*.

'Church', therefore, is far more than buildings and Sunday services. This may come as a surprise to many! That doesn't mean that services and worship are not important. They are central to the being and the doing of Christians. We meet to thank God for his goodness and to praise him for his greatness. We meet to confess our failings and sins and to be reminded of his forgiveness. We meet to learn more of what God is like and of what he can do to and through us. We meet to be reminded that we belong to each other and that we are part of the worldwide fellowship of Christians. All these are big things—but the Church is bigger still.

That is why we must correct those who use the word 'Church' as if it referred only to the clergy. I often hear people talk about friends of theirs who have 'gone into the Church'. What they mean is that their friends have become ministers. Sometimes politicians say, 'Why doesn't the Church say something?' when what they really mean is, 'Why doesn't some bishop or minister say something public?' The fact remains that every time a Christian speaks to someone else, 'the Church' has said something.

Of course, as with any other organized body of people, churches need leaders and those who serve, but clergy exist to serve the Church, not to *be* the Church. The Church is described in the New Testament in words that echo what is said in the Old, namely, that it is the body of people who are themselves a 'holy nation' and a 'royal priesthood'.

'Holy' means 'set aside for special purposes' and 'priesthood' reminds us about the nature of those special purposes. In the Old Testament, priests were those who brought God to the attention of people, and people to the attention of God. They were 'go-between' people. Ever since Jesus Christ, who was supremely the go-between person linking people to their heavenly Father, the Church has been called to be a go-between community.

It is worth remembering that, in spite of all our various denominational labels, there is really only one Church. Those of us who are Anglicans have a long and honoured tradition. In England we are the national church, which carries very big responsibilities. We can sometimes talk as if 'the Church of England' and 'the Church' were one and the same thing. It is good to remember that one of our greatest ever theologians, Richard Hooker, wrote that there was only one Church but that it was like a great sea broken up into inlets and we tended to call these inlets 'churches' when in fact we were really 'societies' within the one Church. Again he noted that we tended to call local congregations 'churches' when they were, in fact, merely assemblies within the society.

It may be a strange way of talking to our ears but the point is important to note. As a member of the Church of England I express my loyalty to the Great One Church of God by trying to be a conscientious member of my own 'society' and 'assembly'. By the same token I need to remember that Christians in other denominations, by being conscientious about being Baptists, Methodists or whatever, are doing exactly the same thing. We may have differences to sort out but we all belong together in God's sight.

This sense of being one Church behind all our differences fits in well with a basic idea that runs through the Bible which is that we are the 'people of God'—the 'holy nation'. We are one because we all recognize that God is our heavenly Father. We are one because we also recognize that Jesus came into the world for all of us and that he died for all of us. Thinking of the great division of his day—that of Jew and Gentile—St Paul wrote:

For [Jesus] himself is our peace, who has made the two one and has destroyed the barrier… His purpose was to create in himself one new man out of the two, thus making peace, and in this one body to reconcile both of them to God through the cross… For through him we both have access to the Father by one Spirit.

Ephesians 2:14–18

So 'Church' is immensely bigger than the little building on the corner where people meet for Sunday services and it is far vaster than a group of men and women who wear clerical collars! It is a worldwide company of people of every race and every section of society that has existed for 2,000 years. You don't 'go to' this sort of Church. You either belong to it or you don't.

But what is it all *for*?

Here another one of the pictures in the Bible is helpful. St Paul described the Church as the 'body of Christ'. What did he mean by that?

To answer that question we must go back to the first Easter Sunday and find ourselves in a crowded room three days after Jesus had been put to death on the cross. The first disciples or followers of Jesus are gathered together feeling discouraged and perplexed. They had seen their hero die on the cross. Now they couldn't even trace his body and complete decent burial arrangements for him. Some of their number—mainly the women—were talking about the grave being empty because Jesus had been raised from the dead. Most of them feel that this is an impossible dream.

Suddenly Jesus is there with them. The door didn't open. No one let him in. They don't know whether to cheer or to cry out in fright. Then Jesus begins to speak. 'Peace be with you,' he says! He shows his wounded hands and side. It is obvious that it really is Jesus! He speaks again: 'Peace be with you. As the Father has sent me I am sending you… Receive the Holy Spirit.'

The reason why the great company of Christians can be called the body of Christ is that the Spirit of Jesus carries on the work of Jesus through ordinary Christian people. The Church exists to be active. We are the body and, individually, the bodies that Christ uses today just as he used his own when he was amongst us. When I was back in my South London Sunday school we sang a chorus about this:

Mine are the hands to do the work
My feet shall run for thee
My lips shall sound the glorious news
Lord here am I, send me.

So this idea of being the body of Christ is a dynamic idea. God looks to our physical bodies to do what he wants to have done in our day and age. The body of Christ is not about 'being' it is about 'doing' and there is so much to be done. Christians working together *are* Christ in the world.

We need to hold this sense of being the body of Christ hand in hand with the other belief about the gift of God's Spirit. He gives his Holy Spirit to the Church and to its individual members to help them to be the arms, legs, mouths, brains, smiling faces and so on that express the personality of Jesus. Our prayer is that others will see Christ in us.

The plain fact of the matter is that if people are to hear what God is saying it will almost certainly be through the speaking and writing of Christians today. Again, if people are to believe that God loves them, the chances are that it will come through the practical caring that is demonstrated by Christians and congregations for those around them. And if our society is ever to become more like the kingdom of God that Jesus talked about, it will happen because those in the churches that have caught something of the vision and values of that kingdom will work and pray in our society to bring about those changes.

All of which brings us back to what baptism and confirmation are about. They are the marking moments of people coming out into the open about being Christian and accepting their responsibility as members of the 'blessed company of all faithful people'. There is no place in the Church for passengers, only for participants. When I come to the end of a confirmation service the blessing that I have to pronounce is straight and to the point. It starts with these phrases:

The Spirit of truth lead you into all truth
Give you grace to confess that Jesus Christ is Lord
and to proclaim the words and works of God...

That is our great calling as the Church. You don't 'go to' a calling. You obey it or you disobey it.

Of course we have different gifts and we are not all able to do everything, but there is always something we can do. I shall never forget a visit, many years ago, to a parish in Liverpool. I was taken to meet one of the great saints of the particular parish church I was visiting. She was an elderly lady who was virtually housebound in the winter. She greeted us warmly and took us through to her little kitchen, which was warm and cosy. The deaconess of the church then said some words that startled me.

'So where are you this morning, Rose?' she said. Back came a reply that I shall never forget.

'South America!' said the little old lady.

Then I saw what she was talking about. On her kitchen table was the magazine and the prayer diary of the South American Missionary Society. She was praying for individual Christian workers by name and asking God's blessing on the various congregations in such places as Argentina, Paraguay, Peru and Chile. I learnt that she divided every day up into times when she prayed in a concentrated way for God to bless the work and witness of worldwide members of the great company of God's Church. She may not have travelled very far from her front door but she was a missionary to the world!

When you take sides for Jesus Christ and become a Christian, you become someone who is *in good company*. Very often the local congregation is tiny and limited in what it can do. The churches of the New Testament era were equally weak. God, however, has a way of proving that he can choose 'the weak things of the world to shame the strong' (1 Corinthians 1:27).

I believe those words. I have seen them proved true. And I have never forgotten that little old lady travelling the world for God in her Liverpool kitchen! I am proud to be in the same good company as her.

4

Living and loving

I remember having lunch with a friend at a pub by the river, and we brought out our coffee and sandwiches and put them down on a table. But it was very wobbly, and not properly balanced, so we had to fold up a paper serviette into a little wad and wedge it under the leg that was short.

The balanced Christian life is a bit like a table with four legs. If one is missing altogether we are in deep trouble. And if all the legs are different lengths then the table—our Christian life—is going to be a very wobbly one.

The four legs are prayer, Bible reading, fellowship and service. All those things also form part of holy communion, or the eucharist, and in the next chapter we shall be looking at that service in some detail—to see how to bring all we can to it, and get the most from it. For now we shall reflect on the four 'legs' that support our Christian life.

Prayer

Prayer is conversation with God. We talk to him about everything that's on our mind and in our heart: about ourselves, and about our friends, and especially about our enemies (if we have any). Jesus gave particular instructions about praying for them, and he gave it in the Sermon on the Mount:

'You have heard that it was said, "You shall love your neighbour and hate your enemy." But I say to you, Love your enemies and pray for those who persecute you, so that you may be children of your Father in heaven; for he makes his sun rise on the evil and on the good, and sends rain on the righteous and the unrighteous.'

Matthew 5:43–45 (NRSV)

It isn't that to love our enemies and pray for them *makes* us children of God, but if we *are* his children then we shall have the same nature as God and act in the same way as he does. And God acts by showering goodness on everyone.

But if we are to pray for those who persecute us, or who are treating us badly, we have to pray honestly. Here is an example of how we might do it.

'Father, I need to pray about this person. I don't feel like praying for him (or for her)—but Jesus told us we had to pray for someone who was behaving very badly towards us. And he has been behaving very badly towards me. I'm feeling very upset and very hurt. Please will you show him what his action has done to me. Show him what he's done wrong—and show me what I've done wrong. [If we are praying something tough for another person it is a good idea to pray the same thing for ourself.] Work in his life, Lord. Let him know how much you love him—and encounter him with your presence. Bless him, Lord, and bless me.'

We might have to pray that prayer day after day—and even year after year, if the thing that was done to us was very terrible. Or if the injury and the hurt was done to someone we love, which is often far harder for us to forgive and to bear. But it's vital to go on praying it.

Forgiveness is one of the key phrases of the Lord's Prayer. 'Forgive us our sins as we forgive those who sin against us.' 'Do the same for me as I am doing for this person who has hurt me,' is what we are saying. And it isn't easy, but no one ever said it would be! But it's glorious—and when we discover what forgiveness and reconciliation are really about we shall find ourselves wondering in amazement at the deep-down peace and happiness that's flooding into our hearts.

Forgiveness is the answer to the child's dream of a miracle by which what is broken is made whole again, what is soiled is again made clean. The dream explains why we need to be forgiven, and why we must forgive. In the presence of God, nothing stands between Him and us—we are forgiven. But we cannot feel his presence if anything is allowed to stand between ourselves and others.

Dag Hammarskjöld, Markings, Faber and Faber

Praying for our enemies is the toughest part of praying. But we've started there because it's such a vital part. Only one part, though, and we're to pray about everything.

'Rejoice in the Lord always,' St Paul wrote to the Christians in Philippi, and to rejoice is to pray. Rejoicing is delighting in God, and praising him just because of the way he is and what he's like. And we know what he's like because Jesus has shown us. 'He who has seen me has seen the Father'—so the Father is a friend of sinners, and sits down to eat with them at parties. Even before they've realized that they're sinners and repented of their sin. It's in the presence of the love of God that they realize their own lack of love—to God and to other people—and then they start to change.

'Again I will say, Rejoice,' went on St Paul. 'Let your gentleness be known to everyone. The Lord is near. Do not worry about anything, but in everything by prayer and supplication with thanksgiving let your requests be made known to God. And the peace of God, which surpasses all understanding, will guard your hearts and your minds in Christ Jesus' (Philippians 4:4–7, NRSV).

The Apostle Paul knew what he was talking about, and he told us to pray about everything. There's nothing that we can't talk to God about—our dreams and our desires (whatever they are); our hopes and our disappointments; all our feelings, of happiness and sadness, and of hatred and anger. Anything and everything—and whatever we try to exclude, God will search out. All the time he'll be shining like light, asking to be allowed into the darkness. So that he can heal and make whole whatever it is that we're hiding away. We may be deeply ashamed of it—but if we let him deal with whatever it is then he'll transform it.

In C.S. Lewis's *The Great Divorce* there is a story of a man who has lust sitting permanently on his shoulder in the shape of a lizard. It keeps whispering into his ear. An angel offers to kill the lizard, and the man anguishes and argues. But finally he gives in.

'Have I your permission?' said the Angel to the Ghost.

'I know it will kill me.'

'It won't. But supposing it did?'

'You're right. It would be better to be dead than to live with this creature.'

'Then I may?'

'Damn and blast you! Go on can't you? Get it over. Do what you like,' bellowed the Ghost: but ended, whimpering, 'God help me. God help me.'

Next moment the Ghost gave a scream of agony such as I never heard on Earth. The Burning One closed his crimson grip on the reptile; twisted it, while it bit and writhed, and then flung it, broken backed, on the turf.

'Ow! That's done for me,' gasped the Ghost, reeling backwards.

For a moment I could make out nothing distinctly. Then I saw, between me and the nearest bush, unmistakably solid but growing every moment solider, the upper arm and the shoulder of a man. Then, brighter still and stronger, the legs and hands. The neck and golden head materialised while I watched, and if my attention had not wavered I should have seen the actual completing of a man—an immense man, naked, not much smaller than the Angel. What distracted me was the fact that at the same moment something seemed to be happening to the Lizard. At first I thought the operation had failed. So far from dying, the creature was still struggling and even growing bigger as it struggled.

And as it grew it changed. Its hinder parts grew rounder. The tail, still flickering, became a tail of hair that flickered between huge and glossy buttocks. Suddenly I started back, rubbing my eyes. What stood before me was the greatest stallion I have ever seen, silvery white but with mane and tail of gold. It was smooth and shining, rippled with swells of flesh and muscle, whinneying and stamping with its hoofs...

The new-made man turned and clapped the new horse's neck. It nosed his bright body. Horse and master breathed each into the other's nostrils. The man turned from it, flung himself at the feet of the Burning One, and embraced them. When he rose I thought his face shone with tears, but it may have been only the liquid love and brightness (one cannot distinguish them in that country) which flowed from him...

C.S. Lewis, *The Great Divorce*, © 1946, published by HarperCollins

We've considered how to pray for our enemies, and how to pray for everything that's in our mind and on our heart. Now we come to the model prayer—the prayer that Jesus taught his disciples when they asked him how to pray.

One way for us to pray it is to use each phrase as the starting point for more praying. So that we say 'Our Father in heaven'—and then stop to let the words and the wonder of them sink into us. When they have done that we go on to the next phrase—'hallowed be your name'. And because we have just been considering the name and the nature of God, Our Father, we deeply desire that name to be hallowed. According to Webster's Dictionary, 'hallowed' means to be greatly respected and venerated—so what we are praying is that his name and nature should be known, and that God should be worshipped and adored.

And so we go on through the whole prayer. If you want to spend some time thinking about how to pray it, you might find it helpful to get hold of *Brushing up on Believing*, which Gavin Reid and I wrote together, because the first six chapters of it are on the Lord's Prayer.

The Lord's prayer is the prayer above all prayers, a prayer which the most high Master taught us, wherein are comprehended all spiritual and temporal blessings, and the strongest comforts in all trials, temptations, and troubles, even in the hour of death.

Martin Luther

Bible reading

If we don't read the Bible and get to know it then our Christian life will be very wobbly indeed. Bible reading is vital to growing at the start of the Christian life, and also to growing up to maturity.

'Let the word of Christ dwell in you richly,' wrote the Apostle Paul to the Colossians (3:16), and the more richly we let that happen the richer our relationship with God is going to be.

The whole point of our Bible reading is to encounter the living God—who loves every one of us with a passionate and enormous love, and longs for us to love him in return. As we read the Bible we shall discover more and more of what God is like—and as the word of God enters deep into our hearts we shall find ourselves being changed, because it is a living word.

'For the word of God is living and active,' the writer of Hebrews tells us. 'Sharper than any double-edged sword, it penetrates even to dividing soul and spirit, joints and marrow; it judges the thoughts and attitudes of the heart' (Hebrews 4:12).

We can start off by setting aside five or ten minutes every day to pray and to read the Bible—and as we start to grow in our spiritual life we shall almost certainly find that the time we spend reading and praying will also grow. On pages 75 and 93 you will find plans for personal morning and evening prayer which Gavin Reid has worked out, and you will see that there is a central place in them for Bible reading. He suggests ways to reflect on the passage you are reading, and gives questions to ask about it.

This is what Archbishop Michael Ramsey wrote about Bible reading:

If we come closer to the inner heart of Bible reading we are not just stuffing our minds with information; we are letting God feed us through his word, and this means letting the scriptures speak to imagination, conscience, feeling, and will, as well as to the mind.

As we read, and read slowly, we pause and let the truth of God come home to us. Our imagination is moved to wonder, *our conscience is pricked to* penitence, *our feelings are moved to* love, *our will is stirred to* resolve, *and our mind to whatever* understanding *we can muster.*

In that way we quietly let the passage of scripture come home to us, mould us, and be our food and drink.

From *Through the Year with Michael Ramsey*,
ed. Margaret Duggan, Hodder & Stoughton

Fellowship

It says in the Acts of the Apostles that the new Christians 'devoted themselves to the apostles' teaching and to the fellowship, to the breaking of bread and to prayer' (Acts 2:42).

That word 'fellowship' is a very important one in the Christian life. The original Greek word *koinoneo* means to have a share in something with someone—and what we are sharing in is Christ himself. *Koinoneo* is about partaking—and 2 Peter 1:4 talks about the promises of God by which we become 'sharers [or partakers] of the divine nature'.

So when Christians get together for fellowship it isn't simply about having a cup of coffee together after church on Sunday, or even having a meal together. It's about talking with one another and sharing with one another all the things that we have been discovering about Christ. It is witnessing to one another about what's been happening in our Christian life—which is the whole of our life, not just the sections of it that have to do with religion, like going to church, reading the Bible, and praying.

Our equivalent of those meetings which the early Christians had is our home group or house group. When we go to church we worship God, we pray, we listen to the Bible being read and expounded, and if we are at holy communion we receive the sacrament of bread and wine. But in the normal church we don't get an opportunity at a Sunday service to have fellowship with one another in the fullest and the biblical sense. Fellowship involves doing things together—common life as well as common talk. So we need to get together with one another and share the things of our faith.

Fellowship has been likened to having a Chinese meal, where we all share in all the dishes. If someone is sad we share in their sadness, and if someone else is happy we share in their happiness. We tell one another what has been happening to us, and what we'd like them to pray for us. We shall study the Bible (our equivalent of the apostles' teaching), and we might spend a certain amount of time in silence, reflecting on what we have been studying, and listening in the quietness for the voice of God. And we shall certainly spend some time praying for one another. We don't have to 'pray out loud' in the way that some people find very difficult—though if that's our way of praying then we can. Those who find it hard can simply mention someone's name, and the fellowship group can then pray for that person in silence.

If there aren't any such groups in your church then you could think about starting one. Find one or two other people, and arrange to meet in someone's home.

Service

> Christ has no body now on earth but yours;
> yours are the only hands
> with which he can do his work,
> yours are the only feet
> with which he can go about the world,
> yours are the only eyes through which his compassion
> can shine forth upon a troubled world.
> Christ has no body now on earth but yours.

Teresa of Avila, a Carmelite nun, wrote those words back in the sixteenth century, and what she said is just as true at the end of the twentieth century. Christianity as it's meant to be is a compassionate and practical religion. It is about doing the right things (and doing them in the right way) as well as believing the right things.

What good is it, my brothers, if a man claims to have faith but has no deeds? Can such faith save him? Suppose a brother or sister is without clothes and daily food. If one of you says to him, 'Go, I wish you well; keep warm and well fed,' but does nothing about his physical needs, what good is it? In the same way, faith by itself, if it is not accompanied by action, is dead.

James 2:14–17

The needs of the world are so vast that we can feel totally overwhelmed. The money we can give to famine relief can seem such a small amount that it hardly seems worth sending it. And very few of us have the inclination or the freedom to work full-time with relief agencies in our own country or abroad. There are homeless people, and hungry people, and people who are depressed and mentally ill.

In Matthew's Gospel, Jesus speaks about the final judgment of all the nations. He is going to be the judge, and he will separate the people 'one from another as a shepherd separates the sheep from the goats'. The separation will be made because of what they have done.

'Then the King will say to those on his right, "Come, you who are blessed by my Father; take your inheritance, the kingdom prepared for you since the creation of the world. For I was hungry and you gave me something to eat, I was thirsty and you gave me something to drink, I was a stranger and you invited me in, I needed clothes and you clothed me, I was sick and you looked after me, I was in prison and you came to visit me."

'Then the righteous will answer him, "Lord, when did we see you hungry and feed you, or thirsty and give you something to drink? When did we see you a stranger and invite you in, or needing clothes and clothe you? When did we see you sick or in prison and go to visit you?"

'The King will reply, "I tell you the truth, whatever you did for one of the least of these brothers of mine, you did for me."

'Then he will say to those on his left, "Depart from me, you who are cursed, into the eternal fire prepared for the

devil and his angels. For I was hungry and you gave me nothing to eat, I was thirsty and you gave me nothing to drink, I was a stranger and you did not invite me in, I needed clothes and you did not clothe me, I was sick and in prison and you did not look after me."

'They also will answer, "Lord, when did we see you hungry or thirsty or a stranger or needing clothes or sick or in prison, and did not help you?"

'He will reply, "I tell you the truth, whatever you did not do for one of the least of these, you did not do for me." '

Matthew 25:34–45

This is a very tough passage, but it is part of what Jesus taught us. You might like to use it for two or three days as the Bible reading for your personal morning prayer—and work with it in the way that Gavin Reid suggests. What does this passage tell me about God? What does this passage tell me about myself and the world in which I live? Is there something I need to learn? Is there something I need to do?

We can't do everything (or very much, for that matter) and with so much need all around us, it's easy to be paralysed. But if we pray for wisdom to know what we can do then we shall certainly be shown. And even the little bit that we can do will make a difference.

In the Gospel of John, a great crowd of people gather around Jesus by the Sea of Galilee, and he says to Philip, 'Where shall we buy bread for these people to eat?'

Philip answered him, 'Eight months' wages would not buy enough bread for each one to have a bite!'

Another of his disciples, Andrew, Simon Peter's brother, spoke up, 'Here is a boy with five small barley loaves and two small fish, but how far will they go among so many?'

Jesus said, 'Make the people sit down.' There was plenty of grass in that place, and the men sat down, about five

thousand of them. Jesus then took the loaves, gave thanks,
and distributed to those who were seated as much as they
wanted. He did the same with the fish.

When they had all had enough to eat, he said to his
disciples, 'Gather the pieces that are left over. Let nothing be
wasted.' So they gathered them and filled twelve baskets
with the pieces of the five barley loaves left over by those
who had eaten.

John 6:7–13

We might not have much to give, but if we hand it
over to Jesus then he will do great things with it. And
we can remember that Christ is on both sides of the
action. We are the body of Christ—and, as Teresa of
Avila said, he has no body now on earth but ours. So we
are Christ in the world.

But Christ is also there *in* the world, 'upholding the
universe by his word of power' (Hebrews 1:3). So if he
is upholding all things and all people by his word of
power he is present in all things and all people. He isn't
the same as them. God is 'wholly other' than his world.
But there is nowhere in the whole universe where God
is not present.

Therefore whatever we do to another person we are
doing to Christ—and whatever we fail to do for them
we are failing to do for him. 'Whatever you did… you
did for me…'

We don't have to get overwhelmed by the vastness of
the task. There are a lot of Christians in the world—
living and loving—and there is something special that
each one of us can do for Christ. An old-fashioned
hymn puts it beautifully and reassuringly.

There's a work for Jesus,
Ready at your hand.
'Tis a task the Master
Just for you has planned.

Haste to do His bidding,
Yield Him service true;
There's a work for Jesus,
None but you can do.

I believe that we discover what we can do as we talk with God and also become aware of our own abilities and our own desires. I don't believe that we have to grit our teeth and do the most unpleasant task that we can possibly imagine. It might be a hard task, but if it is the will of God for us then we shall find that we are enthusiastic about doing it—and the word 'enthusiastic' means 'in God'.

We are living a life in union with God, and we are loving in union with God. He loves us, and we love him, and in the strength and the delight of that love we go out to the world that God loves, to love it and to serve it.

'Go in peace to love and serve the Lord,' is one of the dismissals in the service of holy communion in the *ASB*—and when we hear those words we can know that one way to love and serve the Lord is to love and serve his world.

5

A way to feed on God

'Do this in remembrance of me' Jesus said to his disciples on the night before he died—and ever since then Christians have done what he told us to. We have eaten the broken bread of his body, and drunk the poured out wine of his blood—remembering his words and remembering his sacrifice. 'For as often as you eat this bread and drink the cup, you proclaim the Lord's death until he comes' (1 Corinthians 11:25–26, NRSV).

Now you have been confirmed you can join in the remembrance and in the celebration. Many of us go to the eucharist every Sunday—and it is a great strengthening to our Christian life.

What we shall do in this chapter is to go through Rite A from *The Alternative Service Book 1980*, described as 'The Order for Holy Communion, also called The Eucharist and The Lord's Supper'. It starts with 'the preparation'.

Getting ready: the preparation

We come into the presence of God just as we are, affirming that 'The Lord is here. His Spirit is with us.' There is nowhere in the whole universe where we would not be in the presence of God, but we need to remember it.

The next prayer acknowledges that God sees into all our hearts and knows all our desires.

Almighty God, to whom all hearts are open, all desires known, and from whom no secrets are hidden: cleanse the thoughts of our hearts by the inspiration of your Holy Spirit, that we may perfectly love you, and worthily magnify your holy name; through Christ our Lord. Amen.

It is impossible for us to hide anything from God—and to realize that can be a great relief. We come to him just as we are, and he knows our hearts far better than we know them ourselves. He sees right to the depths of us—and he knows all about our dreams and all about our disappointments. Some of our thoughts are not all they should be, and our minds need to be made clean. So we pray for that to happen, in order that we can love God even more. Then, through us, God will shine out into the world like light in the darkness—and the more we love, the brighter the light will shine.

Saying sorry: prayers of penitence

The second (sometimes fourth) section of the service is about confessing our sins and having them forgiven. The yardstick we measure ourselves by is love, and the two great commandments are the summary of the whole Law:

Our Lord Jesus Christ said: The first commandment is this: 'Hear, O Israel, the Lord our God is the only Lord. You shall love the Lord your God with all your heart, with all your soul, with all your mind, and with all your strength.' The second is this: 'Love your neighbour as yourself.' There is no other commandment greater than these.'

'Amen. Lord, have mercy,' we all say. Webster's Dictionary says that 'Amen' is a word 'used to express solemn ratification (as of an expression of faith) or hearty approval (as of an assertion)'. So we are approving of the commandments—but also asking the Lord God to show forbearance and compassion to us, because although we approve of them we haven't kept them. Perhaps some of us have managed six inches on the yardstick that is love, and some of us a foot. None of us measure up perfectly, and the shortfall is the sin. But so that we don't lose heart some words are read out based on the verse in the Gospel of John which has been called the gospel in a nutshell.

God so loved the world that he gave his only Son Jesus Christ to save us from our sins, to be our advocate in heaven, and to bring us to eternal life.

based on John 3:16

In the light of that love we dare to move on to confession. When we know that we are loved it is easier to be truly honest. The minister says:

Let us confess our sins, in penitence and faith, firmly resolved to keep God's commandments and to live in love and peace with all men.

Then we all say:

Almighty God, our heavenly Father, we have sinned against you and against our fellow men, in thought and word and deed, through negligence, through weakness, through our own deliberate fault. We are truly sorry and repent of all our sins. For the sake of your Son Jesus Christ, who died for us, forgive us all that is past; and grant that we may serve you in newness of life to the glory of your name. Amen.

If you have any difficulties with that confession you can tuck your private prayers in brackets, and pray them silently to God as you are saying aloud the words of the service. That is what I do.

'I am not *truly* sorry,' I say to him, 'although I wish I was, and I pray that you will make me so. And I can't repent of *all* my sins,' I go on, 'because I don't think I really know what they all are. But I pray that you will show them to me—as much as I can bear it.'

All that is often going on inside my head while I am saying the words out loud. It may seem like religious nit-picking—or what other generations of Christians would have called excessive scrupulousness. But the meaning of words matters so much to me that I simply cannot either say them or sing them if they are not true for me.

After we have confessed our sins we hear the words of absolution.

Almighty God, who forgives all who truly repent, have mercy upon you, pardon and deliver you from all your sins, confirm and strengthen you in all goodness, and keep you in life eternal; through Jesus Christ our Lord.

What follows is the Kyrie Eleison, which is the Greek for 'Lord have mercy'. We ask for it three times—praying to the God who is Three in One and One in Three. 'Lord, have mercy', reiterated by the minister and by the congregation. I say the first one to the Father, the second to the Son, and the third to the Holy Spirit—and sometimes the three questions from the service of baptism or confirmation are there in the back of my mind.

**Do you believe in God the Father, who made
the world?**
**Do you believe and trust in his Son Jesus Christ,
who redeemed mankind?**
**Do you believe and trust in his Holy Spirit, who
gives life to the people of God?**

The Gloria comes next—sometimes said and sometimes sung. To say 'Glory to God' is to say 'We praise you, God.' And what we are praising him for is his glory—and the glory of any thing or any person is its real nature and character shining out like light so that everyone can see it.

We have seen the glory of God in the face of Jesus Christ, and the God whose glory we praise is just like Jesus. The friend of sinners who sits down at table and eats with them (and later on in the service something very like that is going to happen). The God who forgives our sins, and who loves us so much that, in order to reconcile us to himself, in Christ he died for us.

Glory to God in the highest, and peace to his people on earth. Lord God, heavenly King, almighty God and Father, we worship you, we give you thanks, we praise you for your glory. Lord Jesus Christ, only Son of the Father, Lord God, Lamb of God, you take away the sin of the world; have mercy on us; you are seated at the right hand of the Father, receive our prayer. For you alone are the Holy One, you alone are the Lord, you alone are the Most High, Jesus Christ, with the Holy Spirit, in the glory of God the Father. Amen.

This section finishes with the Collect, which is a special prayer for that particular week of the Church's year. In the Anglican and Catholic lectionaries (*lectio* = reading) the weeks of the year are divided into the seasons of the Church's year, which means that all the events in the life of Christ and the Church are looked at in order and thought about—and God is worshipped through them and because of them.

The Collect for Maundy Thursday remembers the sacrament that Jesus set up for all time on the night before he died.

Almighty and heavenly Father, we thank you that in this wonderful sacrament you have given us the memorial of the passion of your Son Jesus Christ. Grant us so to reverence the sacred mysteries of his body and blood, that we may know within ourselves and show forth in our lives the fruits of his redemption; who is alive and reigns with you and the Holy Spirit, one God, now and for ever.

Listening to God: the ministry of the word

We are in the presence of God, who loves us and forgives us. All the words spoken in the service so far have deepened our awareness of God and said something about the nature of God. Now there are more words, read out of the Bible, and preached from the pulpit.

We can listen expectantly, praying that God will speak to our hearts. And if we listen in the right way he almost certainly will. As we allow the life-giving word of God to penetrate our hearts through our open ears we shall not only pray 'Your will be done.' We shall know what the will of God is, and be given the strength to go out and do it.

Two or three readings from the Bible—Old Testament, Epistle and Gospel—and sometimes (but rarely in practice) a Psalm. If we are really going to 'let the word of God dwell in [us] richly' (which we were thinking about in the last chapter) we shall read the Bible for ourselves as well as hearing it read to us on Sundays. When I became a Christian I couldn't put it down. I read it at home and on trains and on boats—and the whole book became alive.

The Reverend John Collins, who had shown me how to become a Christian, had told me to pray and to read every day, and to underline the verses which were special and important to me. I still have that first Bible. It is worn out now, with its pages falling out. But I still dip into it sometimes, because I have a special affection for it. And as I turn over the pages of the New Testament and get to the letter which Paul wrote to the Romans I smile. Almost all of it seemed important and special to me (it still does!), and almost all of it is underlined.

Daily Bible reading is a vital part of our spiritual food—and if you aren't already doing it then with all my heart I recommend that you start. When Jesus was tempted by the devil in the desert he was hungry.

The tempter came to him and said, 'If you are the Son of God, tell these stones to become bread.' Jesus answered, 'It is written: "Man does not live on bread alone, but on every word that comes from the mouth of God." '

Matthew 4:3–4

In that context, God's words meant scripture, and Jesus fought off Satan every time with words from the Old Testament. In the description of the armour of God in Ephesians 6:10–18 Paul writes of 'the sword of the Spirit, which is the word of God', and we can use it to fight with just as Jesus did—as well as feeding our souls on it.

There is always an Epistle and a Gospel reading at the eucharist (though sometimes an Old Testament reading is substituted for the Epistle). So here is one of each—with some of the ways that God can speak to us through the words. For you there will be other ways as well, and as the words are spoken we can listen attentively and use our imagination to see the scenes and the pictures they describe.

The Bible never speaks in abstract concepts, so (even if the preacher does!) we can always find something to see in our mind's eye for us to meditate on.

The epistle to the Hebrews (4:12–16) gives us another picture of a sword and then talks about the high priesthood of Jesus.

For the word of God is living and active. Sharper than any double-edged sword, it penetrates even to dividing soul and spirit, joints and marrow; it judges the thoughts and attitudes of the heart. Nothing in all creation is hidden from God's sight. Everything is uncovered and laid bare before the eyes of him to whom we must give account.

Therefore, since we have a great high priest who has gone through the heavens, Jesus the Son of God, let us hold firmly to the faith we profess. For we do not have a high priest who is unable to sympathise with our weaknesses, but we have one who has been tempted in every way, just as we are—yet without sin. Let us then approach the throne of grace with confidence, so that we may receive mercy and find grace to help us in our time of need.

As we let God search our hearts with his word we can be trustful, because it is love who wields the sword. The whole point of the divine heart surgery that pierces our hearts is to make them beat with a stronger love. So that we can love God and other people more deeply.

God enters into our heart—and we can enter into the heart of God. That is what it means for us to approach the throne of grace through Jesus the Son of God. The high priest went into the Holy of Holies just once a year, carrying a sacrifice for the sins of the people. Then he came out again. But Jesus, our great high priest, has gone into the real presence of God on our behalf, and he is there for ever. One who has the same nature as us is there, for us, in the holy presence of God. So we can come to the heart of God with utter confidence, knowing how much he loves us, and knowing that we are forgiven and understood.

After the Epistle, the Gospel—and we stand while it is read to show our recognition of the wonder of it. 'Glory to Christ our Saviour,' we say when it is announced to us, and, 'Praise to Christ our Lord,' when it is finished. We have to allow him to be our Saviour before we can acknowledge him as Lord, because our broken relationship has to be mended before we can adore him and serve him.

Then Jesus said to his disciples, 'If anyone would come after me, he must deny himself and take up his cross and follow

me. For whoever wants to save his life will lose it, but
whoever loses his life for me will find it. What good will it
be for a man if he gains the whole world, yet forfeits his
soul? Or what can a man give in exchange for his soul?'

Matthew 16:24–26

The way to listen to those words in a life-giving way
is to look at the pictures. In your mind's eye, see Jesus
taking up his cross. Pick up a heavy, wooden cross
yourself, and put it on your shoulder. Follow Jesus, and
realize where he is leading you. You are not just on a
demonstration with the cross as the banner. You are
going to be crucified. In Luke's Gospel it says 'daily'—
that you are to take up your cross day by day and be
put to death on it.

But all that will die is your false self. If you try to save
that self you will never find your true self. You could try
to stay a shining, brown conker, polishing yourself more
and more desperately as day by day you grow old and
wither. Or you could fall into the ground and die. Then,
one day, you will become a great chestnut tree with
spreading branches, glowing in the spring with pink
and white candle flowers. But then you will have to take
up your cross again—because for there to be yet more
fruit even those flowers will have to die.

The sermon comes next, with more listening to the
word of God. The New Testament sees preaching as a
vital and essential ministry—but it is the message
rather than the preacher that is important. 'For we do
not preach ourselves,' Paul wrote, 'but Jesus Christ as
Lord, and ourselves as your servants for Jesus' sake.
For God, who said, "Let light shine out of darkness,"
made his light shine in our hearts to give us the light of
the knowledge of the glory of God in the face of Christ.
But we have this treasure in jars of clay to show that
this all-surpassing power is from God and not from us'
(2 Corinthians 4:5–7).

Every preacher is jar of clay—a candlestick holding the light of God—and if people are to come to the light out of the darkness they must hear the good news preached to them.

And how can they believe in the one of whom they have not heard? And how can they hear without someone preaching to them? And how can they preach unless they are sent? As it is written, 'How beautiful are the feet of those who bring good news!'

Romans 10:14–15

I love the idea of the preacher being a candlestick, and I love candles. I once read a beautiful passage about candles in a children's book by William Raeper, called *Warrior of Light*. The children and their uncle are in a fight against the powers of darkness, and the dark shadows are trying to get into their house. So they light candles and put them in every window.

The candles burned. Where their light fell the shadows melted and vanished. There was something more than candle-power here, something old and deep that went back to the beginning of the world.

Maddy watched the points of living flame. There was something so tremendous in the light that you felt very small beside it. The flame was pure and dissolved the darkness. It was alive, like a heart, like life, like hope. And Maddy sensed the pain as well as the power in the flame—it was wounded as well as triumphant. The sheer goodness of the flame, the life of the light, beckoned her, was ready to welcome her.

'You see, don't you,' said Uncle Alistair, 'the Light invites—it does not compel. Because its power comes out of suffering and is used with understanding.'

'But they're candles!' said Maddy.

'What did I tell you before?' said Uncle Alistair. 'The

candles represent — they show *— what's really happening.
And that's something we can't usually see: the Light is
greater than all the powers of darkness.'*

*Steadily the candles burned. Slowly they turned back the
tide of darkness. The shadows retreated. Light swallowed
the darkness, as if the shadows had never been.*

'The light shines in the darkness,' said Uncle Alistair,
'but the darkness has not overcome it!'

William Raeper, Warrior of Light, Lion, pages 94–95

The sermon shines with the light of Christ crucified—
and reflects and magnifies for us some truth of the good
news of the love of God, Father, Son and Holy Spirit. We
then stand up and declare our faith in that God, and the
Nicene Creed (like the other Creeds) is a summary of
the great truths of the Christian faith. It helps sometimes
to take just one phrase from the Creed and spend some
time reflecting on it and exploring it.

As I reflect now on the start of it, and make it mine,
'*I* believe in one God', I feel a fresh awareness dawning
within me of the glory and greatness of the God who
holds all things in being. The words of the Jewish
Shema come into my mind: 'Hear O Israel: the Lord our
God, the Lord is one…' I look at the young poplar tree
in my garden as the wind gently moves its branches,
and I look beyond it to the hill and to the sky. And I
reflect on the unity of all things… and the fact that in
Christ the one God made all things, and the words of
Colossians start to stir in my mind.

*He is the image of the invisible God, the firstborn over all
creation. For by him all things were created: things in
heaven and on earth, visible and invisible, whether thrones
or powers or rulers or authorities; all things were created by
him and for him. He is before all things, and in him all
things hold together. And he is the head of the body, the
church; he is the beginning and the firstborn from among*

the dead, so that in everything he might have the
supremacy. For God was pleased to have all his fulness
dwell in him, and through him to reconcile to himself all
things, whether things on earth or things in heaven, making
peace through his blood, shed on the cross.

Colossians 1:15–20

'I believe in one God'—and that's the God I believe
in! I couldn't remember all the words of Colossians,
only some of them. So I looked them up to write them
down. And now I am feeling a deep sense of wonder at
the glory of the one God I believe in, and that we believe
in. And perhaps tomorrow I shall reflect on the next two
words in the Creed—'I believe in… the Father'.

There isn't space here to go all through the Creed,
but over the coming months you might like to try the
same exercise, and reflect on one phrase a week.

Speaking to God: the intercessions

The intercessions come next in the service, when we
pray for all the aspects of God's world and our world.
For the Church, the rulers of our nation. For all nations
and for all people, including ourselves. C.S. Lewis used
to see this part of the service as a framework upon
which he could hang his own prayers. I find that
helpful. Otherwise I find some of the prayers too vast
for me to make any sense of praying them.

I cannot manage 'God bless Africa', but if someone
says that, then I will let the face of an African leader
come into my mind, and pray and ache for him.

Some people would prefer the Church of England
prayers to be freer at this point. But a living spirituality
is about working with things as they are and not as we
would like them to be. Working out ways of being able
to pray with what we've got and are given—not with
what we haven't got and aren't being given. We *are* the
body of Christ when we are praying, and we *are*

praying in the Spirit (because as Christians we are in Christ, and the Spirit is in us). So if we stay there and don't fret, then that is what we are meant to be doing at that point in the service.

After the intercessions we have the prayers of penitence, if we didn't pray them earlier. Then, sometimes but not always, the prayer of humble access.

We do not presume to come to this your table, merciful Lord, trusting in our own righteousness, but in your manifold and great mercies. We are not worthy so much as to gather up the crumbs under your table. But you are the same Lord whose nature is always to have mercy. Grant us therefore, gracious Lord, so to eat the flesh of your dear Son Jesus Christ and to drink his blood, that we may evermore dwell in him and he in us. Amen.

A lot of people love that prayer—but some people have certain difficulties with it, and the phrase they can have trouble with is the one that says, 'We are not worthy so much as to gather up the crumbs under your table.'

But to say that doesn't mean that we are worth*less*. Christianity tells us just the opposite to that. One meaning of 'worthy' according to Webster is 'having worth or value'—and Jesus said that our soul or our true self was worth more than the whole world.

The word 'worthy' in the prayer of humble access is used in its other meaning, of 'meritorious'. So we are saying to God: 'We know that we aren't here because of our merit or our goodness—but we're here because you created us and you love us and you are merciful.' We don't come to the table of the Lord because of what we have done, but because of what he has done.

For it is by grace you have been saved, through faith—and this not from yourselves, it is the gift of God—not by works, so that no-one can boast. For we are God's

workmanship, created in Christ Jesus to do good works,
which God prepared in advance for us to do.

Ephesians 2:8–10

The ministry of the sacrament

We start off this section with the Peace. Reminding ourselves that:

Christ is our peace. He has reconciled us to God in one body by the cross. We meet in his name and share his peace.

Sometimes we 'share the peace' and sometimes we don't. Occasionally I have been set upon by a stranger and hugged and kissed, which I don't like very much. I used to be attached to Southwark Cathedral, and at this point in the service the President would come down from the communion table with another minister (sometimes me, if I was deacon) and 'give' the peace to the two people at the end of every row along the aisle. Then it would be passed along the row from person to person—'Peace be with you... And also with you'. It is the peace that comes from Christ that we are symbolically sharing in—not a general hugging and kissing by the congregation—and to make it a bit more formal can make the theological truth more effectively.

The preparation of the gifts

The bread and wine are placed on the holy table if they were not already there, and the offerings of the people are collected and presented. A time to think about gifts and giving: God's gift of himself to us—and our gifts to God.

Yours, Lord, is the greatness, the power, the glory, the splendour, and the majesty; for everything in heaven and on earth is yours. All things come from you, and of your own do we give you.

The eucharistic prayer

Then we move on to the great eucharistic prayer. We hear the familiar words, telling us the wonderful story of the setting up of the sacrament. We listen again to the glorious events of the birth and the life, and the death and the resurrection of Jesus Christ. As we listen, attentively and expectantly, we can be caught up into worship and wonder. Sometimes one phrase will touch us especially… and one that I love is 'our duty and our *joy*…'

For he is your living Word; through him you have created all things from the beginning, and formed us in your own image…

It can be almost too much glory to take in, so we can let the words carry us along and let God do with us what he wants. Words that tell the story, and when we hear the story we praise God for it, and remember our Saviour Jesus Christ:

Who in the same night that he was betrayed, took bread and gave you thanks; he broke it and gave it to his disciples, saying, 'Take, eat; this is my body which is given for you; do this in remembrance of me.' In the same way, after supper he took the cup and gave you thanks; he gave it to them, saying, 'Drink this, all of you; this is my blood of the new covenant, which is shed for you and for many for the forgiveness of sins. Do this, as often as you drink it, in remembrace of me.'

We follow that with another affirmation of our faith: 'Christ has died: Christ is risen: Christ will come again', we all say.

The great prayer goes on, remembering.

Therefore, heavenly Father, we remember his offering of himself made once for all upon the cross, and proclaim his mighty resurrection and glorious ascension. As we look for his coming in glory we celebrate with this bread and this cup his one perfect sacrifice. Accept through him, our great high priest, this our sacrifice of thanks and praise; and as we eat and drink these holy gifts in the presence of your divine majesty, renew us by your Spirit, inspire us with your love, and unite us in the body of your Son, Jesus Christ our Lord. Through him, and with him, and in him, by the power of the Holy Spirit, with all who stand before you in earth and heaven, we worship you, Father almighty, in songs of everlasting praise.

The words we then say to praise God are like the words of the angels and the elders and the living creatures round the throne of God in the vision that is the book of Revelation—so we are joining in the worship of heaven (just as we were earlier when we cried out 'Holy, holy, holy Lord!'). Now we say:

Blessing and honour and glory and power be yours for ever and ever. Amen.

At this point we say the Lord's Prayer. 'As our Saviour taught us, so we pray…' A reminder that we are the family of God and that God is our Father. We pray this prayer as the sons and daughters of God, and, because we know the wonder of having our own sins forgiven, we forgive other people in the same way. If we aren't forgiving them we don't stop being the children of God. But we do stop enjoying it, because there is a cloud between us and our heavenly Father.

If we are having real difficulty in forgiving someone then we have to do what Jesus told us to do in the Sermon on the Mount. 'I tell you: Love your enemies and pray for those who persecute you…' (Matthew 5:44). So during the service we can pray for them. We can tell God how they have hurt us, and why we are finding it so hard to forgive—and we can ask him to make them realize why we are hurt, and also ask him to bless them.

One way to prod ourselves into forgiving is to remember what Jesus said just after he had taught the disciples the Lord's prayer: 'For if you forgive others their trespasses, your heavenly Father will also forgive you; but if you do not forgive others, neither will your Father forgive your trespasses' (Matthew 6:14–15, NRSV).

Forgiving is never easy and it always costs a great deal. Our forgiveness cost Jesus his life.

Forgiveness breaks the chain of causality because he who 'forgives' you—out of love—takes upon himself the consequences of what you have done. Forgiveness, therefore, always entails a sacrifice. The price you must pay for your own liberation through another's sacrifice, is that you in turn must be willing to liberate in the same way, irrespective of the consequences to yourself.

Dag Hammarskjöld, *Markings*, Faber and Faber, 1964

After the Lord's Prayer there is the breaking of the bread, and the reminder that 'Though we are many, we are one body, because we all share in one bread.'

The time has now come for the congregation to share the bread and the wine, remembering all that it means. We are invited to receive:

Draw near with faith. Receive the body of our Lord Jesus Christ which he gave for you, and his blood which he shed for you.

As we wait to go up and receive the bread and wine we can pray and we can meditate. Perhaps praying for someone or something very important to us. Holding the person or the situation in our hearts as we go up. Or perhaps we want to remember the setting up of the sacrament in that room in Jerusalem the night before Jesus died, and to strengthen our faith as we remember the truths and the facts of our faith.

The Christian faith is rooted in history. Events took place. A baby boy was born. The lame walked, the blind saw again, the hungry were fed—and a man died on a cross. If we had been there we would have seen the events happen.

Peter's second letter testifies that what the apostles preached and wrote was the truth. They hadn't made it up.

For we did not follow cleverly devised myths when we made known to you the power and coming of our Lord Jesus Christ, but we had been eyewitnesses of his majesty.

2 Peter 1:16

They were eyewitnesses too of the setting up of the sacrament—and if we had been in the Upper Room on that night we would have seen what Jesus did and heard the words he said. The disciples didn't invent them or make them up.

'Take, eat; this is my body which is given for you; do this in remembrance of me…' 'Drink this, all of you; this is my blood of the new covenant, which is shed for you and for many for the forgiveness of sins.'

Words spoken in Aramaic at an evening meal nearly 2,000 years ago. A meal that really happened. Not a cleverly devised myth. Imagine the meal—and think about the meaning. Reflect on the symbolism of the lamb. Think about sacrificial lambs, and about the Lamb of God. 'Behold the Lamb of God, who takes away the sin of the world' (John 1:29). Then:

Eat and drink in remembrance that he died for you, and feed on him in your hearts by faith with thanksgiving…

The body of Christ keep you in eternal life.

The blood of Christ keep you in eternal life.

Through the eating of the bread and the drinking of the wine our faith is strengthened, and we have a fresh realization that Christ is in us. St Paul wrote about 'Christ in you the hope of glory'—and we believe that. And the bread and the wine are within us, being transformed into us. And Christ is in us, transforming us into himself and feeding our spiritual life.

After we have been given the bread and the wine we go back to our place and pray, sitting or kneeling. Reflecting on the wonder of the gift—of God-in-Christ giving himself to us to feed on. Our own deep thankfulness and delight is gathered up in the words of the next prayer, and we offer ourselves to do the will of God in the power of God.

Almighty God, we thank you for feeding us with the body and blood of your Son Jesus Christ. Through him we offer you our souls and bodies to be a living sacrifice. Send us out in the power of your Spirit to live and work to your praise and glory.

Refreshed and sent out again

Then we are dismissed in the peace of God, and blessed with the blessing of God. A peace for our hearts and our minds that comes from the presence of God with us and through knowing God. A peace that we can know even when our hearts are breaking and our own little world seems to be falling apart. The blessing of God, which is God-in-Christ coming to us and giving himself to us in love. The God who is love. Love for us to live off and to feed on. God himself—the source of our life and our being, our joy and our deep heart-peace.

The peace of God, which passes all understanding, keep
your hearts and minds in the knowledge and love of God,
and of his Son Jesus Christ our Lord; and the blessing of
God almighty, the Father, the Son, and the Holy Spirit, be
among you, and remain with you always.

'Amen,' we say to that.

Then we hear the final words.

'Go in peace to love and serve the Lord,' says the one
who is officiating. And we respond with the words. 'In
the name of Christ. Amen.' So now we go out into the
world in the peace of Christ—in company with the
living God who gives himself to us, and who took flesh
and died in order to do it. We go out into a lost world
that is dying in the darkness. But it is still God's world.
He created it and he loves it.

In the service we remembered our own coming home
from the far country, as prodigal sons and prodigal
daughters. And we prayed for the ones who are still out
there in the darkness. For myself, the words that come
immediately after communion in the Anglican service
are often the words that I take out as my own prayer for
God's beloved world.

Father of all, we give you thanks and praise, that when we
were still far off you met us in your Son and brought us
home. Dying and living, he declared your love, gave us
grace, and opened the gate of glory. May we who share
Christ's body live his risen life; we who drink his cup bring
life to others; we whom the Spirit lights give light to the
world. Keep us firm in the hope you have set before us, so
we and all your children shall be free, and the whole earth
live to praise your name; through Christ our Lord. Amen.

6

Personal morning prayer

A simple Daily Office

Begin in relaxed silence for a minute.

> For the rest and safety of the past night
> *I thank you, Lord.*
> For all that this new day will bring
> *I trust you, Lord.*
> For all that is wrong in my life
> *Forgive me, Lord.*

Praise and adoration

Read (aloud if possible) the words of a favourite hymn or one of the Psalms on page 77.

Bible reading and reflection

Begin by saying the following prayer:
> *Open my eyes to your Word.*
> *Open my mind to your Word.*
> *Open my will to your Word.*
> *May I hear you and obey.*

Read your Bible passage and reflect upon it. If you are not using a Bible reading system with comments and notes, ask yourself the following questions:

1. What does this passage tell me about God?
2. What does this passage tell me about myself and the world in which I live?
3. Is there something I need to learn?
4. Is there something I need to do?

Silence

Our Father in heaven
hallowed be your name
your kingdom come
your will be done
on earth as in heaven.
Give us today our daily bread.
Forgive us our sins
as we forgive those who sin against us.
Lead us not into temptation
but deliver us from evil.
For the kingdom, the power,
and the glory are yours
now and forever. Amen

Intercessions

It is helpful to keep a notebook or list for matters that should be remembered in your prayers.

Reflect quietly on the names and issues on your list, remembering that God is aware of your thoughts and concerns. Remember to thank him for the good things that come to mind!

Dear Father
thank you for being with me in my prayers,
help me to remember
that you are with me for the rest of this day.
Amen.

This is the day that the Lord has made!
I will rejoice and be glad in it!

7

Psalms for use in daily prayers

Day	Psalm	Day	Psalm
1	1	17	95
2	3	18	96
3	8	19	98
4	16	20	100
5	19	21	103:1–17
6	23	22	111
7	24	23	115
8	33:1–11	24	119:1–8
9	34:1–8	25	121
10	36:5–10	26	123
11	40:1–8	27	124
12	46	28	125
13	67	29	145:1–13
14	71:1–15	30	146
15	84	31	150
16	90:1–12		

Life for ever: I Peter

Many people find it helpful to use Bible notes as part of their daily prayers, either in the morning or the evening. So here are fourteen days of readings out of 1 Peter–the first letter, or epistle, written by the Apostle Peter to the early Church.

This letter is full of encouragment and hope, written from a pastor's heart to people who were facing persecution. Some modern scholars think that Peter is a pseudonymn, and that his name was attached to the letter, as was the custom in those days. It wasn't dishonest—more a way of giving credit where credit is due. These were Peter's ideas and teaching passed on to another church leader, so it was Peter's name that went along with them.

One of the reasons for thinking that Peter didn't write it is that it is such superb Greek, and a Galilean fisherman would not have been able to write it. But other scholars think that Peter did write it, through the Sylvanus he mentions at the end of the letter. Peter thought it—and Sylvanus scribed it, and corrected and polished the style as he did so.

This is a lovely letter, and it is possible that it was regularly used to prepare adult candidates for their baptism. So it is a good letter to read immediately after your confirmation. It is about a life that lasts forever. The eternal life that begins in this life, in a living relationship with the living God, and continues after death in the presence of God and the glory of heaven.

God so loved the world...

Peter, an apostle of Jesus Christ, To the exiles of the Dispersion in Pontus, Galatia, Cappadocia, Asia, and Bithynia, chosen and destined by God the Father and sanctified by the Spirit for obedience to Jesus Christ and for sprinkling with his blood: May grace and peace be multiplied to you.

Peter was a Jew, one of God's chosen people. Jews have sometimes asked ruefully, 'Chosen for what? Chosen for trouble?' The trouble about being chosen by God is that there is a responsibility attached to it—to make the glory of God known over all the earth. Generally speaking the Jewish nation failed to tell out the glory of the love of God. The reluctant prophet Jonah was very displeased when God didn't pour out judgment on non-Jewish Nineveh, who repented after Jonah's warning: '...is not this what I said when I was yet in my own country?... I knew that thou art a gracious God and merciful, slow to anger, and abounding in steadfast love, and repentest of evil' (Jonah 4:2).

But the tender Jewish prophet Isaiah looked ahead to the day when through the suffering servant of God the light of the love of God would shine in the whole world: 'It is too light a thing that you should be my servant to raise up the tribes of Jacob... I will give you as a light to the nations, that my salvation may reach to the end of the earth' (Isaiah 49:6, RSV).

Now it was happening. Now the Jew Peter could speak of the Gentiles in terms that once he would only have applied to Jews. Once it was the Jews who were the exiles of the dispersion. Now it was the Gentiles. Once it was the Jews who were chosen by God. Now it was the Gentiles. God had always intended it so. Now, through the Jew who shed his blood on Good Friday, the Gentiles could be sprinkled with the blood of sacrifice, just as the Jews had been on the great Day of Atonement each year.

A prayer

Father God, thank you for loving me, for choosing me, for sanctifying me, and for forgiving me. Help me to obey you, together with all the members of your church. 'May we whom the Spirit lights give light to the world.'

No more decay

Blessed be the God and Father of our Lord Jesus Christ! By his great mercy we have been born anew to a living hope through the resurrection of Jesus Christ from the dead, and to an inheritance which is imperishable, undefiled, and unfading, kept in heaven for you, who by God's power are guarded through faith for a salvation ready to be revealed in the last time.

In our Western world death is something that we hide behind the closed doors of a refrigerator. We never see the decay and decomposition of a dead body. In the ancient world the unacceptable fact of death could not be hidden. 'He will be stinking by now,' they said to Jesus when he told them to roll away the stone from the front of Lazarus' grave. He wasn't stinking, because Jesus had called him forth from the grave to live again, and he walked out swathed in his grave clothes. But one day he would die again, and his body would go through the processes of decay that all bodies are subject to.

One day we shall all have to walk into the valley of the shadow of death. But it will make all the difference in the world if we know that the Lord who conquered death is our shepherd. It is far better for us than it was for the Jews. Later on in their history they started to believe in the resurrection of the dead—and out of the depths of his despair Job had cried out in faith that one day it was going to happen: 'I know that my Redeemer liveth, and that in my flesh shall I see God.' But the rest of the ancient world was without hope, and death was the end.

Into that desolation the Christian hope of eternal life shone like a great light in the darkness. A Christian had a new relationship with the living God and Father of our Lord Jesus Christ, and because of the resurrection he (and she—because women had a new status because of Christianity) had a new and living hope. The body would die, but it would be raised up to an endless life, imperishable and incorruptible.

A prayer

Thank you so much, Lord Jesus Christ, for the difference that your death makes to mine.

More precious than gold

In this you rejoice, though now for a little while you may have to suffer various trials, so that the genuineness of your faith, more precious than gold which though perishable is tested by fire, may redound to praise and glory and honour at the revelation of Jesus Christ. Without having seen him you love him; though you do not now see him you believe in him and rejoice with unutterable and exalted joy. As the outcome of your faith you obtain the salvation of your souls.

Those early Christians were facing terrible trials. A vital, living Christianity always makes itself unpopular, because it turns the world's values upside down and makes a radical demand on people to change. Everyone doesn't want the love and forgiveness of God—because before they can know the joy of forgiveness they have to admit that they need it. And to respond to the love of God is a risky business. Because it will change us—from one degree of glory to another. 'Though you do not now see him you believe in him and rejoice with unutterable and exalted joy.' Yet with the eyes of faith we do see him. 'All we, with unveiled face, beholding as through a glass the glory of the Lord, are changed into his likeness, from one degree of glory to another.' Beautiful—but also frightening—and people run away from the light into the darkness. They have persecuted the children of light all through the centuries. Some years ago, most of the Christians in Eastern Europe were coming out of a persecution and daring to worship openly again. But they had suffered for many years and their faith had been tested like gold in a crucible of fire. Gold won't last for ever. But their faith, and ours, will—and our hope, and our love. For ever and ever.

A prayer

Lord Jesus Christ, when my faith is tested, help me to realize that its genuiness is being tested like gold in a fire. Help me to hold on and to trust you, whatever happens. And I pray for those whose faith is being tested at the moment…

Tell out the glory

The prophets who prophesied of the grace that was to be yours searched and inquired about this salvation; they inquired what person or time was indicated by the Spirit of Christ within them when predicting the sufferings of Christ and the subsequent glory. It was revealed to them that they were serving not themselves but you, in the things which have now been announced to you by those who preached the good news to you through the Holy Spirit sent from heaven, things into which angels long to look.

We have been thinking about the fact that the whole of the Jewish nation had refused to let the glory of God shine over all the earth, but had wanted to keep the glory for itself. But there were great and beautiful exceptions to that generalization and the prophets were some of them. The Jewish nation had been specially chosen by God and he had set his love on them. But God has made us free men and women, and we can choose the level of our response when someone sets their love upon us on a divine or a human level. If you have ever loved someone who rejected your love, you will know what I am talking about. You are helpless to do anything except to go on loving and praying. God has made every human being free, to accept or reject love, and to accept or reject him. The prophets did not reject him or his love. They hungered and searched and longed for God—for the God who had set his love on them. To entangle the two threads is impossible. Barclay says that 'God's truth comes only to the man who searches for it,' that 'inspiration comes when the revelation of the Spirit of God meets the searching of the mind of man. In all inspiration there is an element which is human and an element which is divine; it is the product at one and the same time of the search of the mind of man and the revelation of the Spirit of God.'

A prayer

Father, thank you for the faithfulness of your prophets. May I not hold lightly those things that they longed to know about and to understand. Help me, in my small way, to preach the good news to my generation.

Think!

Therefore gird up your minds, be sober, set your hope fully upon the grace that is coming to you at the revelation of Jesus Christ. As obedient children, do not be conformed to the passions of your former ignorance, but as he who called you is holy, be holy yourselves in all your conduct; since it is written, 'You shall be holy, for I am holy.' And if you invoke as Father him who judges each one impartially according to his deeds, conduct yourselves with fear throughout the time of your exile.

The men of the Middle East wore long, flowing robes. These protected them from the heat of the sun but made it difficult to be physically active. So they would tuck their robe into their girdle—'gird it up'—to let their loins and legs be free and active. That is what Peter is telling Christians to do with their minds. Take whatever steps are necessary to use their minds effectively to the glory of God— effectively to love God. 'Be transformed by the renewing of your mind,' St Paul wrote, and the mind is an essential part of Christian growth as well as Christian worship. Sometimes teachers say to their pupils, in some desperation, 'Think!' It has a powerful effect—and everything in all creation started as a thought in someone's mind, either God's or ours.

The sister of a brilliant professor that I know told me that when he was a little boy the family would find him sitting on a blanket box at the top of the stairs looking out of the window, and they would ask, 'What are you doing, Donald?' 'I'm thinking,' he'd say, 'just thinking.' He spent hours of his life doing it—and while most of us are not in his category, it is still crucial to use our mind in our Christian lives. We shall not be able to set our hope fully on the grace that is coming to us if we don't know what that grace is. So we need to find out.

A prayer

*Father, you have given me my mind. Help me to use it…
to worship you.. to study your word… to meditate on you and on your truth… to contemplate your creation… and to praise you because of all these things. Help me to use my mind to the praise of your glory. Amen.*

The Passover lamb

You know that you were ransomed from the futile ways inherited from your fathers, not with perishable things such as silver or gold, but with the precious blood of Christ, like that of a lamb without blemish or spot. He was destined before the foundation of the world but was made manifest at the end of the times for your sake. Through him you have confidence in God, who raised him from the dead and gave him glory, so that your faith and hope are in God.

At the start of John's Gospel John the Baptist sees Jesus coming towards him and cries out, 'Behold, the Lamb of God, who takes away the sin of the world.' Later in that gospel Jesus is killed on the cross at the same time as the Passover lambs are killed and eaten in the great Feast of Passover which is taking place in Jerusalem. That feast looked back to the Exodus from Egypt. Before they set out, a family took a lamb, and killed and ate it. They put its blood on the top of their doorposts, so that when the angel of the Lord came to kill the firstborn sons in Egypt he would see the blood and pass over that house. So the blood, according to the Jewish story, speaks to us of safety from death and also of a setting free from slavery.

They were slaves in the land of Egypt. We are slaves to sin— which means that there is that power or principle of sin in us which masters us, and in one sense we enjoy being mastered by it. The epistle to the Hebrews speaks of enjoying 'the pleasures of sin for a season'. But only for a season. They don't last— and we end up being destroyed by them, just as a drug addict is destroyed by the drug she starts off by delighting in but ends up being totally captive to. The blood of Christ ransomed us from all that, and from the futile ways that we walk in simply because we are members of the human race. 'As in Adam all die, so in Christ shall all be made alive.'

To think about

'The one final and utter failure of the church would be its ceasing to be able to bring sinners assurance of forgiveness.'
Leonard Hodgson, *The Doctrine of the Atonement*

Born for love

Having purified your souls by your obedience to the truth for a sincere love of the brethren, love one another earnestly from the heart. You have been born anew, not of perishable seed but of imperishable, through the living and abiding word of God; for 'All flesh is like grass and all its glory like the flower of grass. The grass withers, and the flower falls, but the word of the Lord abides for ever.' That word is the good news which was preached to you. So put away all malice and all guile and insincerity and envy and all slander. Like newborn babes, long for the pure spiritual milk, that by it you may grow up to salvation; for you have tasted the kindness of the Lord.

All creatures have the same nature as their parents, whether the creature is a tiny blackbird chick just hatched out a turquoise spotted egg, or a foal that stands on its legs and nuzzles its mother only minutes after it is born; or a human baby, totally dependent for life on another human being. Christians, born again of the Spirit of God, have the nature of God. And the nature of God is love. It is impossible for a real Christian not to love, because the new nature growing within her (or him) is the same as God's nature. But the new nature has to grow, just as a baby has. The newborn Christian is to thirst for the pure spiritual milk of the 'word'. That isn't just the Bible. It is all things that have to do with the Word, who is God himself. The Word that went forth from God on the first day of creation... the Word who was 'in the beginning with God'... the word that the whole of creation declares about the glory of God without even speaking a word. The word of the Lord abides for ever—and it is through that word that the Christian is born.

A prayer

Living Lord God, help me to nourish your life in me—and to thirst for all things that flow from you, the living Word. Help me to live—to love you and my neighbour and myself, with the love that flows from your heart of love.

A precious stone

Come to him, to that living stone, rejected by men but in God's sight chosen and precious; and like living stones be yourselves built into a spiritual house, to be a holy priesthood, to offer spiritual sacrifices acceptable to God through Jesus Christ. For it stands in scripture: 'Behold, I am laying in Zion a stone, a cornerstone chosen and precious, and he who believes in him will not be put to shame.' To you therefore who believe, he is precious, but for those who do not believe, 'The very stone which the builders rejected has become the head of the corner,' and 'A stone that will make men stumble, a rock that will make them fall'; for they stumble because they disobey the word, and they were destined to do.

Next door they are building a house and the work suddenly slowed down. So I went to see why. The builders told me they were getting the corners right. If they don't, the house will start to lean like the tower of Pisa. So the quoin at the corner of each line of bricks is the crucial brick. In an arch it is the stone in the middle that takes all the thrust of the sides and holds them together. That is what Jesus is for Zion.

Once upon a time there was a city divided by walls into four parts. In one part all the people and animals and houses were red, in another green, in another blue and in another yellow. All the people thought their colour was the best and they never spoke to each other. But one morning the red people found a great black stone in their midst. They painted it red, but the paint wouldn't stick. So one night they threw it over the wall to the green people—and the green people threw it over over to the blue—and the blue to the yellow. The stone wouldn't change. It stayed obstinately and beautifully black. But the people started to change. They climbed up their walls and started to talk about the problem of the stone. And they enjoyed talking, so they started to knock down the walls. Then they used the bricks to build a church, within a great fourfold arch, at the centre of the new city. And the cornerstone of the arch was the great black stone.

Royal bridgebuilders

But you are a chosen race, a royal priesthood, a holy nation, God's own people, that you may declare the wonderful deeds of him who called you out of darkness into his marvellous light. Once you were no people but now you are God's people; once you had not received mercy but now you have received mercy.

We have just thought about building houses and now it's bridges. One of the Latin words for priest is *pontifex*, which means a bridgebuilder. Bridges get us from one place to another and the traffic can go both ways—in this case from God to man and from man to God. In Old Testament times it was only the high priest who could go in to the presence of God, once a year, bearing the blood of a sacrifice killed on behalf of the people. The New Testament uses all the Old Testament imagery to say that Christ has changed that situation once for all. When Christ died, the way into the presence of God was open for ever. Christ went into the presence of God through his own blood. We who are Christians are 'in Christ', baptized into Christ, and in Christ we live in the presence of God. In Old Testament ritual that presence was 'within the veil'. The veil separated the presence of God from the people of God—and Matthew's Gospel tells us that it was 'torn in two from top to the bottom' at the very moment that Christ died. The epistle to the Hebrews speaks of the 'high priesthood of Christ'—who is alive for ever to make intercession for us. And we who are in Christ share in the priesthood. All Christians are members of a royal priesthood—bridgebuilders—to bring God to men and women, and men and women to God— in our prayers and in our conversation.

A prayer

Lord God, help me to realize that in Christ I am a member of a royal priesthood—a royal priest. May I indeed declare your wonderful deeds to those who are sitting in the darkness and sorrow of sin—so that they too may come and live in the marvellous light of your love. May I bring you to men and women—and men and women to you.

All sins spoil...

Beloved, I beseech you as aliens and exiles to abstain from the passions of the flesh that wage war against your soul. Maintain good conduct among the Gentiles, so that in case they speak against you as wrongdoers, they may see your good deeds and glorify God on the day of visitation. Be subject for the Lord's sake to every human institution, whether it be to the emperor as supreme, or to governors as sent by him to punish those who do wrong and to praise those who do right. For it is God's will that by doing right you should put to silence the ignorance of foolish men. Live as free men, yet without using your freedom as a pretext for evil; but live as servants of God. Honour all men. Love the brotherhood. Fear God. Honour the emperor.

The last sentence of this passage is astonishing, because Peter was almost certainly talking about Nero—and telling the Christians to honour him. Perhaps to treat a man with respect and honour is to open up a possibility of drawing him back up the slope again, however far down he has gone. 'The passions of the flesh' are far more than just sexual sins. Galatians 5 lists them and contrasts them with the fruit of the Spirit: 'Now the works of the flesh are plain: fornication, impurity, licentiousness, idolatry, sorcery, enmity, strife, jealousy, anger, selfishness, dissension, party spirit, envy, drunkenness, carousing, and the like. I warn you, as I warned you before, that those who do such things shall not inherit the king-

dom of God. But the fruit of the Spirit is love, joy, peace, patience, kindness, goodness, faithfulness, gentleness, self-control.' In his superb book *The truth about AIDS*, Dr Patrick Dixon is very clear that people who have caught AIDS through their own sexual sin are not worse sinners than those of us who sin other sins. All sins of the flesh war against the soul and they are all destructive, to the sinner and to those that he or she sins against.

A prayer

Holy Father, help me to realize what the sins of the flesh really do to me, to other people, and to you.

Even when it's unjust...

Servants, be submissive to your masters with all respect, not only to the kind and gentle but also to the overbearing. For one is approved if, mindful of God, he endures pain while suffering unjustly. For what credit is it, if when you do wrong and are beaten for it you take it patiently? But if when you do right and suffer for it you take it patiently, you have God's approval.

This is one of the toughest passages in the New Testament—on a par with loving our enemies and doing good to those who hate us and despitefully use us, which Jesus told us to do in the Sermon on the Mount. In Rome slaves did all the work—including being teachers and doctors and musicians and actors. Sometimes the slaves were much-loved members of the family they worked in—but in law they had no status. A slave was just a thing, not a person. Slaves had no human rights because they were not regarded as human. They knew they were in their hearts. They were bound to, because every human being is made in the image and likeness of God. And now Christianity had told them that what they hardly dared to believe was true—that in Christ, 'There is neither Jew nor Greek, there is neither slave nor free, there is neither male nor female; for you are all one in Christ Jesus' (Galatians 3:28, RSV).

So now what? Were they to band together and revolt? They could have taken over Rome if they had. But Peter says, 'No'. Treat your masters with all respect—not just the kind ones but the cruel ones as well. Why? Because in Christ's passion and suffering the glory of God shone out into the darkness of the world with a brightness that had never been seen before—the glory of God in the face of Christ crucified. In their own small way that is what the slaves of Rome were called to do. In our even smaller way so are we.

A prayer

Lord Jesus Christ, teach me what it means to endure pain while suffering injustice. May I know the power of your resurrection and the fellowship of your suffering.

Don't hit back

For to this you have been called, because Christ also suffered for you, leaving you an example, that you should follow in his steps. He committed no sin; no guile was found on his lips. When he was reviled, he did not revile in return; when he suffered, he did not threaten; but he trusted to him who judges justly. He himself bore our sins in his body on the tree, that we might die to sin and live to righteousness. By his wounds you have been healed. For you were straying like sheep, but have now returned to the Shepherd and Guardian of your souls.

Humanly speaking it is an impossible standard we have been set—and without the Spirit of Christ within us it would be impossible to contemplate it. The world answers back and fights back when it is attacked. We are told not to—because Jesus didn't. When I am driving and an aggressive driver tries to cut me up by passing me on the wrong side, my natural reaction is either to accelerate and stop him getting in, so that he squeals to a stop, or if he happens to manage it then I give him a long sustained hoot. Not always, but more often than I should. The Spirit of Christ is having a battle with me about it—and only sometimes winning it. But I am convinced of the rightness of the theory, even if I only sometimes put it into practice.

Living as Christ lived is to let the evil come to a halt in our own body. It is to take it into ourselves and not to hit back. Christ took all the evil of the whole world into his own body on the tree—so that we might stop sinning and hating and start living and loving. Really living. Really loving. He was wounded. We are healed because of it. We were lost like sheep. Now the shepherd has found us and rescued us. But it cost him all he had.

A prayer

Lord Jesus Christ, help me more and more to see the glory and the wonder of the way you lived. Help me not to fight back when people (and drivers) annoy me. Help me to accept their evil and let it stop in me—so that it doesn't go any further. Give me your Spirit to be my helper, day by day.

The winning jewel

Likewise you wives, be submissive to your husbands, so that some, though they do not obey the word, may be won without a word by the behaviour of their wives, when they see your reverent and chaste behaviour. Let not yours be the outward adorning with braiding of hair, decoration of gold, and wearing of fine clothing, but let it be the hidden person of the heart with the imperishable jewel of a gentle and quiet spirit, which in God's sight is very precious. So once the holy women who hoped in God used to adorn themselves and were submissive to their husbands, as Sarah obeyed Abraham, calling him lord. And as you are now her children if you do right and let nothing terrify you.

In the ancient world women did not have any rights. Legally their status wasn't much better than slaves. In Jewish Law a husband owned his wife in the same way that he owned his cattle (hence 'Thou shalt not covet thy neighbour's wife… nor his ox…'). Women were not supposed to take decisions for themselves, but now some women were. They were deciding to become Christians. So Peter told them to be submissive. If they hadn't been they could have been divorced (or if they were Romans, put to death). But they were also to be good wives. The theological reasons why slaves and women had to be patient and passive under suffering were that Christ had been, and by his passion he let the glory of God shine out into the world. A Christian wife's behaviour would do the same thing—and her husband might be won for Christ by the transformation of her character. Many wives spent their time concentrating on their clothes and their hairstyles. But there was to be a different sort of adorning for the Christian woman. A quiet and gentle spirit. She wasn't to go around looking frumpish. That wouldn't have brought glory to God—and would have annoyed her husband.

A prayer

Thank you, Lord Jesus Christ, that you came to set the whole human race truly free—including women and slaves.

Five vital virtues

Finally, all of you, have unity of spirit, sympathy, love of the brethren, a tender heart and a humble mind. Do not return evil for evil or reviling for reviling; but on the contrary bless, for to this you have been called, that you may obtain a blessing. For 'He that would love life and see good days, let him keep his tongue from evil and his lips from speaking guile; let him turn away from evil and do right; let him seek peace and pursue it. For the eyes of the Lord are upon the righteous, and his ears are open to their prayer. But the face of the Lord is against those that do evil.'

Unity of spirit is not an optional extra but absolutely essential. Sections of the Church disagree on important issues. But we shall only glorify the name of Christ if we love one another and affirm the truths which we do believe in common. We are to be sympathetic: with all the sin and sorrow of the world, we are to weep with those who weep and rejoice with those who rejoice, because we can feel their sorrows with them and feel their joys. When someone is desperately sad, sometimes all we can do is to sit in silence and somehow suffer with them. We are to love our brothers and sisters in the faith: to want the best for them and to pray for the best. We are to have a tender heart. Perhaps to allow ourselves to feel the suffering of the world and to pray and take action when we see hungry, weeping children, and hear of people

dying and being hideously crippled on the roads, because we drive so selfishly. Finally, we are to have a humble mind, or humility, which comes from realizing that we are creatures and that God is our creator. We couldn't create a fly, let alone the worlds—and it is God in Christ who holds the worlds and us in existence.

To think about

Spend some time reflecting on the five Christian qualities of unity, sympathy, love, compassion and humility, and consider how developed each one is in your own life.

9

Personal evening prayer

A simple Daily Office

Begin with relaxed silence for a minute.

Think back over the day, remembering that God is aware of your thoughts.

> For your companionship throughout this day
> *I thank you, Lord.*
> For those acts and thoughts
> that have let you down
> *Forgive me, Lord*
> As I face the hours of this night
> *Be with me, Lord*

Praise and thanksgiving

Read and reflect on one of the following Bible passages:

Psalm 23	Matthew 6:25–34
Psalm 103:1–17	Luke 2:29–32
Psalm 146	Romans 8:35–39
Isaiah 40:25–31	Philippians 2:5–11
Matthew 5:3–10	Revelation 21:1–4

Prayer

Reflect quietly on the names and issues on your daily prayer list.

Lighten our darkness
Lord, we pray;
and in your mercy defend us
from all the perils and dangers of this night;
for the love of your only Son,
our Saviour Jesus Christ. Amen
(from ASB)

Heavenly Father
here I am at the day's end
tired and facing the dark hours of the night.
Thank you for being with me
throughout this day
for loving me
helping me
and being patient with my failures.
Grant me the rest I need for my body, my mind
and my emotions.
Give me the inner stillness
that comes from knowing that
I am perfectly safe in your arms;
and keep me mindful
that you will be there for me tomorrow.
Amen.

If you have enjoyed reading and using *Confirmed for Life* and the notes on 1 Peter, you may wish to know that BRF produces a regular series of Bible reading notes, *New Daylight*, which is published three times a year (in January, May and September) and contains printed Bible passages, brief comments and prayers. *New Daylight* is edited by Shelagh Brown and is also available in a large print version.

Copies of *New Daylight* may be obtained from your local Christian bookshop or by subscription direct from BRF (see over).

For more information about *New Daylight* and the full range of BRF publications, write to: The Bible Reading Fellowship, Peter's Way, Sandy Lane West, OXFORD OX4 5HG (Tel. 01856 748227)

SUBSCRIPTION ORDER FORM

Please send me the following, beginning with the Jan/May/Sep* issue:

Qty

____ New Daylight   £8.55 p.a.   _____

____ New Daylight large print   £12.00 p.a.   _____

*delete as appropriate

All prices include postage and packing.

Please complete the payment details below—all orders must be accompanied by the appropriate payment—and send your completed order to **BRF, Peter's Way, Sandy Lane West, Oxford OX4 5HG**.

Name . . . .

Address . . . .

. . . . Postcode . . . .

Signed. . . . . Date . . . .

Payment for subscription(s)   £ _____

Donation   £ _____

Total enclosed   £ _____

Payment by cheque □ postal order □ Visa □ Mastercard □

Expiry date of card . . . .

Signature . . . .

(essential if paying by credit card)

BRF is a Reg. Charity (No. 233280)   CFL

NB *New Daylight* may also be obtained from your local Christian bookshop—ask at your local shop for details.